Negotiate to Close

How to Make More Successful Deals

Gary Karrass

SIMON AND SCHUSTER

NEW YORK

Copyright © 1985 by Gary Karrass
All rights reserved
including the right of reproduction
in whole or in part in any form
Published by Simon and Schuster
A Division of Simon & Schuster, Inc.
Simon & Schuster Building
Rockefeller Center
1230 Avenue of the Americas
New York, New York 10020

SIMON AND SCHUSTER and colophon are
registered trademarks of Simon & Schuster, Inc.
Designed by Irving Perkins Associates
Manufactured in the United States of America

10 9 8 7 6 5 4 3 2 1

Library of Congress Cataloging in Publication Data
Karrass, Gary.
   Negotiate to close.

   Includes index.
   1. Selling.   2. Negotiation in business.   I. Title.
HF5438.25.K37   1985   658.8'5   85-10846

ISBN: 0-671-55483-2

Acknowledgments

I owe an immense debt of gratitude to the many hundreds of business people who attended the Effective Negotiating and Effective *Sales* Negotiating seminars I have conducted over the past ten years, and so willingly shared their experience with me and their seminar groups.

I am indebted, too, to my father, Dr. Chester L. Karrass, designer and planner of the Effective Negotiating® seminar. His many years of practical experience and his pioneering research into negotiation formed the foundation for my own work in the field.

Gary Karrass

Contents

Introduction

The False Assumptions That Hold You Back

Read this book and you'll make better deals.

And you'll do it in a way that makes you and the other person happier, makes your boss happier, makes your company more profitable, and makes your paycheck fatter.

You'll do this because you'll be a better negotiator.

You don't think of yourself as a negotiator? Neither did I, years ago. I thought negotiation was something reserved for diplomats and labor relations people. Then I realized I was kidding myself. I was negotiating all the time. Even when I was dealing in a fixed-price product, I was negotiating. I was negotiating time, or volume, or terms, or delivery, or service, or advertising, or add-ons, or throw-ins, or any one of a dozen other things that can be involved in a sale.

How well I negotiated these had as much effect on profit as price negotiating. Sometimes more.

I was negotiating in other ways, as well. I negotiated performance with employees, raises and promotions with employers. I negotiated with people of other departments in my organization. I negotiated whenever I bought or sold a car or a boat or a house or any one of scores of other things.

We all negotiate and we all spend a great deal of time at it.

This book covers the strategies, tactics, techniques, and skills of negotiation—how to use them and how to deal with them. It covers countless negotiation situations where these things come into play.

Specifically, this book is aimed at people who want their business to do better: company presidents, sales people, sales management, and general management people. They know that better negotiation means better sales and better sales mean better business. But the negotiation situations we deal with come up in all occupations, regardless of business or profession, and in our personal lives as well.

So what's in this book applies to everyone.

Did you ever lower a price before the buyer asked you to? Sure, most of us have. Ever get trapped by the "ballpark quote for planning purposes only"? Of course. Ever go into a negotiation convinced the competition could kill you? You knock down your price to rock-bottom, then discover later you were the only one who had what the buyer needed? I can almost see you nodding.

This book will help you avoid these and the hundred other mistakes we've all made. This book will help you understand and get rid of those false assumptions that hold you back, and once held me back.

Think about this: *During the few minutes you'll take to read this introduction, millions of negotiations will be taking place all over the world.* Buyers will be buying and sellers will be selling everything under the sun—apples to airplanes, computers to carloads of grain, swimsuits to skyscrapers.

Some sales people will do a terrific job of negotiating, profitable for themselves and their organizations, and leave a satisfied customer behind to boot. Other sellers will do an extremely poor job, leaving behind profit that was there for the asking, or the taking.

We're going to talk about the methods of the first group—those sales people who do extremely well. And how they do it. Effective Negotiating is a skill, and one that can be learned. Easily.

We're going to talk about negotiation strictly from the sales person's point of view. I'll tell you why.

The sales person is in a terrible position in negotiation—*because he thinks he is.* The buyer always has a lot more clout—*because he thinks the buyer has more clout.*

These ideas are wrong. But this is how the sales person sees negotiation. And seeing is believing.

This book will change your mind. You'll view negotiation differently, you'll do it more effectively. And you'll do it without worrying about getting ulcers.

You'll learn that you are in a strong position, and that you have many sources of power—some of which have never occurred to you. You'll learn that there are countless ways to use these powers in negotiation.

It's critical that you know about these powers and how to take advantage of them in negotiation. Why? Because virtually everything in your sales experience, and a few things that you learned in sales training, work *against* your being a good negotiator.

Not long ago someone said this to me: "Negotiation is

simple. A buyer and a seller get together, they quibble about price, then they make a deal. Right?" Wrong. Negotiation is aggravating, tense, makes us anxious and nervous. It's more personal than objective, often illogical, with little respect for procedures, rules, and regulations. It's a process, during which all kinds of things happen and all kinds of things change. It's an experience in human relations, no more subject to the laws of accounting than to the laws of physics.

You've seen the customer who paid top dollar come out of negotiation all smiles, and for good reason. And you've seen the one who got the lowest price come out grumbling, also for good reason.

The sales person with the least competition and the best product may go to the negotiation table feeling powerless; the sales person surrounded by keen competition may deal from a surprisingly strong power base. A sales person may *lose* a sale by lowering a price—or *win* one by resolving not to lower it.

This kind of thing happens all the time in negotiation and there are perfectly obvious reasons why it does.

You're going to learn here about making assumptions, always a tricky business.

There was a time when I went through the day carrying a heavy sack of assumptions over my shoulder, most of them all wrong and the rest of them mostly wrong. You're probably lugging similar erroneous assumptions around. And the sack gets heavier all the time.

Let's look at some of these assumptions and how they stack up against the facts of the matter:

1. The buyer is all-powerful, holding all the cards.
   Fact: He rarely, if ever, is, or does.

2. The buyer knows what he wants. Fact: Sometimes he does, sometimes he doesn't, no matter how detailed the specifications may be.
3. You'll make the sale solely on the basis of price. Fact: Price is the most overrated word in negotiation.
4. Your competition is all around you, with better products and better prices. Fact: This is almost never the case.
5. You'd close more sales if you had more authority. Fact: In most negotiations you'd be better off with less authority.
6. Your only real weapon is the ability to lower the price. Fact: Price-cutting is only one of dozens of negotiation tools at your command, and many are more effective than price-cutting.

These are just some of the false assumptions you'll have to clear out of your mind to make room for what I have to say about the sales person's real powers—the most important part of this book.

Early in the game I walked around grossly underestimating my powers, and just as grossly overestimating the buyer's powers. I changed that and it wasn't hard because power is in the head. You can change it, too.

You have the power of *commitment*—one that has characterized some of the most successful sales people in business history. The power of being willing to *risk*—to gamble for a bigger pot. The power of *legitimacy*, the power of *wooing*, the power of *knowledge*, even in some circumstances the power of your *competition*. And you have the power of *time*—a key to your other powers.

If you're a sales manager or sales executive you have another power, and responsibility. That is to constantly fortify, reinforce, and enhance the powers of your sales people. In other words, to build their psychological muscle.

When was the last time a buyer told you he had only a certain amount in his budget? Probably yesterday. Or asked you what-if he bought ten instead of five? Or went on and on in conversation about how great your competitors are, what terrific features their products have? We've all heard these things a thousand times.

They're tactics—just a few of the big bagful of tactics the buyer has and uses, all day long.

We're going to explore those tactics thoroughly, explain them, dissect them. Then we'll explore the countermeasures you have. And there are many countermeasures for each tactic.

I've been teaching sales negotiation for ten years. Not long ago I ran into a word processing systems salesman who had attended one of my seminars.

He said this to me:

"Since taking your course I look at myself and my position, the buyer, and the entire negotiation in a whole different way. When the buyer uses one of his tactics, even though what he says may be true, I see it as a tactic, I identify what tactic it is. Then I buy some time—usually talking about anything but price—and I sort out in my mind what I can do, what measure I can take, to counteract his tactic. Then I make the judgment and do it. It's not that I don't believe him—if he says he only wants to spend so many dollars, for example. It's more like, what can I do to help him change his mind in the next few minutes, or the next few hours. Maybe I end up having to lower my price. But I go down a lot of other avenues before I do that, and often I don't have to lower the price. If I can get him enticed enough, he'll up his dollar figure."

That salesman learned, as you will, that negotiation is a game. A serious game, certainly, and sometimes a very serious game. But still a game and best handled that way. Played.

The buyer isn't an enemy. See him as an adversary and you bring hostility to the table. You shorten or close communication. You cripple your own powers, and your ability to pick up information and more information—so important in negotiation.

Think of the buyer as the other player, the guy across the chess board, on the other side of the net. He makes a move or takes a shot and you spot it, consider it, then deal with it. Effectively.

There's nothing difficult about becoming a good negotiator. You recognize your powers—really understand that you have them. You recognize the tactics that buyers use, day after day. You become aware of the countermeasures that are there for you to use to deflect those tactics. And you use them.

You'll learn in this book about the shifting targets of negotiations, the changing truths . . . what kind of satisfaction buyers really seek . . . how to use aspiration levels to your advantage . . . how to preserve the long-term relationship, if you're on the inside, and how to break it, if you're on the outside . . . how to make concessions the smart way, always getting something in return . . . how to negotiate within your own organization . . . and many more things.

Stick with me through these pages and you'll be a better negotiator. Being a better negotiator is the shortest and straightest road to closing more sales—better sales.

I

Unlocking Your Negotiating Strength

1

How Your Job Works Against You

Aim high and you'll come out better. Ever heard that? Sure. We've all heard it a hundred times. We tell it to our children.

Ask for more, you'll get more. Right? Certainly. Everyone knows that. But is it true in negotiation?

Let me tell you about Howie Hendricks, my first boss. Howie is the president of a construction company that does large masonry jobs. My first job was selling for him.

If Howie figured a job at $90,000, including a good profit, he'd price it at $100,000. His sales people argued with him. I argued with him. Why risk losing the job? Why not go in with the $90,000?

"Mr. Hendricks," one of us would say to him, "if everything goes well, there's profit in the $90,000, and Brock Masonry is hungry and is bidding already."

"Listen," Howie would reply, "sometimes things don't go right. If you ask for $90,000, nobody's going to offer you $95,000 or $91,000 and you'll never discover if you could have gotten that extra $5000 or that extra $1000— and that extra is nothing but profit.

"If you ask $100,000 you can always go down, but if you ask $90,000, you can't go up."

Howie's sales people were as intelligent as he was. And most of them were as knowledgeable as he was. We did most of the selling, most of the negotiating. Why didn't we want to ask for more? I, and the others, figured that $90,000 was better than no job at all. We didn't want to take a chance of losing the sale. Most of us felt lucky to get the job at $90,000. If the buyer was skilled, we felt lucky to get it at $89,000. If the buyer was really persistent, we felt lucky to get $88,000.

Howie understood: if you aim higher, you come out better. If you ask for $100,000, you have a chance of getting more than $90,000. And it worked that way. Howie usually didn't get the $100,000. But he usually got more than $90,000. And everything over the $90,000 was pure profit.

In my seminars I ask the group the question: "If you aim higher, do you come out better?" Every person in the room agrees you do.

It's even been proven in scientific experiments.

At Harvard Graduate School of Business Administration researchers put up a partition in the middle of a small room. Hundreds of people negotiated, two at a time—one coming in one door, the other coming in the other door.

Half the negotiators were told the typical bargainer in their position got $7.50. The other half were told $2.50. What did they average? $5? No way.

The ones who aimed for $7.50 got about that, those who aimed for $2.50 got about that. And it came out that way time and time again.

In another experiment, done by Dr. Chester L. Karrass, 120 professional negotiators were paired off to negotiate a lawsuit. The outcome? Those who aimed for $700,000 or more averaged $650,000. Those who aimed for less than $700,000 averaged $425,000.

Again, you ask for more, you get more.

But if we all agree that's true, why do we hesitate, resist asking for more? Why don't we get more?

If you're a sales manager, how often has a sales person called you up and said this: "Gee, the product's really good. I think we ought to raise the price 30 percent, or 20 percent."

If you're a sales person, have you ever called headquarters to complain the new price increases are too low? I can almost hear you laughing.

Why is it funny? You aim higher, you come out better. Ask for more, you get more. True, right? It's funny because we who sell spend most of our time discovering the *least* we'll settle for—not the *most* we can get.

Why? Because our jobs train us—to be poor negotiators. Our jobs train us day after day, week after week, month after month, to believe that the prices the product manager has given us are just too unrealistic, just too high.

Our jobs as sellers knock our aspiration levels down, way down. And because of this, we not only don't see the powers we have in negotiation—we don't even take the time to look for them.

How does it happen? I'll show you. We're going to spend a typical week with my friend, Charlie Miller. A lot of Charlie's experiences are familiar to me, and will be familiar to you—very familiar. Charlie Miller sells a line ranging from desktop copying machines to large electronic printing systems. He was back at his desk after a two-day sales meeting at the home office. It was a good meeting. The bigshots were encouraging, and realistic. He thought back for a minute . . .

"Sales are holding up, and the company is doing well for these economic times," the president, Sam Wilkinson, had said. "We have no big expansions planned, but no cutbacks either. That isn't bad, for these days."

"We're holding our own against the competition from the technical standpoint," Henry Reisman, the development vice president, had said. "And we have new features in the pipeline that will enhance our products, features that will help you sell, features based on real customer wants and needs."

"Manufacturing costs are up but we're committed to hold the line as long as we can on price increases," the marketing chief, George Smith, had said.

All in all, Charlie felt pretty good as he left his office that first day: cheerful, optimistic, and positive.

This was good because he had an important appointment later that week. It was with Amkey, Inc., a small wholesale company, but one that needed an entire new reproduction system for its corporate offices—one involving multiple machines, small to large.

He'd done a lot of homework for this one. And his systems people had really supported him. They'd gone in and done a workflow study, mapped out a plan for the machine network, helped him pinpoint its advantages in terms of efficiency and economy. His proposal was a thorough one. The price looked a little high going in, but he had shown how it would cost-justify itself in a very short time. The customer had been sitting on the proposal for two weeks. The meeting later this week would be a go or no-go decision.

In the meantime, he had other calls to make. He headed for his car.

At the first place, a chemical company, Charlie cooled his heels for nearly an hour before the buyer, all apologies, called him in. Then the buyer called in two of his associates to listen, too.

Five minutes into his pitch (they had expressed interest in four copying machines), the buyer was called out for a phone call, and never reappeared. Ten minutes later, one of the associates excused himself, saying he had to make another meeting. Charlie did the last ten minutes for the other associate, who looked so young he probably didn't have the authority to buy a box of paper clips.

The young associate smiled at him. "Gee, we sure appreciate your coming by, Charlie. But the prices, they're more than we figured. We just don't have the budget for anything like that. I guess we'll look into having the old machines overhauled. Thanks for taking the time to see us."

Well, you can't win them all, Charlie thought, as he threw his briefcase into the backseat of his car and headed for his next call.

It was different this time, but not much better.

"Charlie," the buyer told him, "I hate to tell you but your competitors are all over the place, and they've got some interesting features—things you don't have, Charlie.

"One of them has that new collating system; it's the fastest I've ever seen. Automatic stapling at no extra charge. And those fellows are ready to deal. They're ready to sharpen their pencils. We're just going to have to look around some more. We'll let you know."

The next prospect was the corporate office of a pest control company. The lead passed on to Charlie said they were in the market for a couple of desktop copying machines and, possibly, a small printing system.

The buyer, a cold-mannered man, never moved a muscle while Charlie was explaining his products, then outlining his proposed solution to the customer's needs. Charlie got down to his price for the machines, threw in a ten percent discount, and leaned back in his chair.

The buyer looked at Charlie and said one sentence: "You've got to do better than that." Then he shook Charlie's hand, and turned away.

Charlie stood there for a few seconds. "I'll call headquarters when I get back to the office . . . see what I can do."

"You do that," the buyer replied, without turning his head.

Next morning Charlie was on the phone in his office with the product pricing manager in the home office.

"Give me the go-ahead for another ten percent and I can get this exterminator outfit. It's worth it, Joe. It's three copiers and a printing system. And the company's growing. They'll need more stuff."

"Did the guy say he'd close if you gave him ten percent more?"

"Not exactly," Charlie replied. "But I know that'll do it. He just has to feel he got a better discount than the other guy. They're going to need more machines, Joe. I can see it coming. We can lock them in."

The pricing manager thought for a minute. Then: "Charlie, I'll give you eight percent. It's not good business, Charlie. It's a favor. If the profit's not there, why bother to sell it? Why bother to deliver it? But take the eight, Charlie. And good luck."

Charlie thanked him and hung up. The guys in head-quarters, he thought. They're good guys. But they don't know what the business is all about. They're not out here, where the rubber meets the road. They don't know how fast the competitors are improving their products, and knocking down the prices. They ought to spend some time out here where the business is.

Charlie called the buyer at the exterminating outfit with the good news about the additional eight percent discount. His reply took Charlie aback. "Thank you for going to the trouble, Mr. Miller. But we've decided to farm out all our printing and copying. It will cost more, we realize that. But we're short of space. We don't really want those machines cluttering up the place. But thank you again."

At his next stop, visiting a customer who already had several of his company's machines and needed two more, Charlie automatically threw in the extra eight percent discount—and made the sale.

"We know your machines are okay because we have them," the buyer said. "But there are a lot of okay machines around now. And your prices are a little high. I probably could have done better, even considering your so-called extra discount. I just can't take the time now to shop around; I have too many other things to do, more important things."

That Friday morning Charlie went to his office thinking about his appointment that afternoon with Amkey. It was an important one—the one that could put him into his company's Quota-Plus Club. He wasn't going to blow it.

He'd made 11 calls so far that week. One of the other calls turned out to be a fair-to-middling prospect, maybe in a month or so. One other turned into a sale, for several small machines. He'd felt pretty good about that one. Then when the buyer shook his hand, he said, "You ought to tell your shipping people, Charlie. The reason we went with you was that you were the only one who could meet our delivery schedule."

Charlie loosened his tie, put his feet up on his desk, and leaned back. His mind went back to the sales meeting he'd attended the week before. They'd better get in gear with those new features, he thought. Do they really *know* how fast the competitors are moving their new features and add-ons into the market? And price increases? They'd better hold the line, or they'll price us right out of the market. Why don't they give us more clout with the pricing? We're out here, we're doing the business. We know what's going on. Why do we have to run to headquarters like kids for permission to knock the price down a little more than the routine discount?

Times are hard, the economy's down—that's all we hear all day long. The customers are pinching pennies. Don't they understand that at the home office? They're trying to do their jobs. But they should spend a little time out here, in the real world. Find out what it's really all about. How do they price, anyway? Do they build in half a buck so the research guys can have a court to play volleyball on at lunchtime?

Charlie sat forward, leaned down, and pulled his Amkey proposal from his briefcase. He thumbed through it. It was a good job, he thought. The people at sales school would love it. But did the customer read it? Did they read half of it . . . any part of it? Or did they just look at the bottom line?

At twenty past two that afternoon Charlie was sitting

in the Amkey lobby—still waiting to be called for his two o'clock appointment with the office manager and the buyer. He had noticed when he signed in that two of his competitors had been there before him. Had Amkey already given one of them the order? Were they just going through the motions with him, getting enough quotes to satisfy their procedures?

I may even be just wasting my time here, Charlie thought. They probably need some feature we don't have yet, something our development guys are still playing with. We've cost-justified the hell out of our price, but did they even notice that? They probably think our price is too high. It is, I've thought that all along. They'll pick, pick, pick at the price and I'm not supposed to lay any more discount on it. I had to fight for the 14 percent that's there now. But that's the only way I'll get the order, getting the price down. Amkey knows that. They can just sit it out, and end up getting what they want at a better price . . . from somebody.

Charlie made a decision. His branch manager wouldn't be happy about it. The pricing guy at headquarters would blow his stack. He'd make less commission, but he'd make the Quota-Plus Club. Most important: he'd stand a chance of closing the sale.

The secretary beckoned to Charlie and he stood up and went into the private office. The office manager and the buyer were seated at the table, Charlie's proposal in front of them. They stood and shook hands agreeably.

Charlie sat down and smiled. "Gentlemen, I have good news. I've been arguing with headquarters all week and they finally agreed. I can shave another nine percent off the bottom line."

Fifteen minutes later a happy Charlie left Amkey with

the signed contract in his briefcase and the appointments scheduled for the first installation and employee training sessions.

As you were sure to notice, the Charlie who went to Amkey that Friday was in a far different frame of mind than the Charlie who had started the week—fresh from a sales meeting, optimistic, positive, feeling good about his company and his products.

What happened between Monday and Friday?

His job, that's what happened. The very nature of his job (which was not going to change, any more than it would change for any sales person) worked against him. It undid everything his company and his managers and executives had worked so hard to do at the sales meeting. It turned him from positive to negative. It knocked the wind out of his confidence in his company, his proposal, his products, his prices. And it did this even though Charlie had a pretty good week in terms of sales, even before the Amkey deal.

Let's take a look at Charlie's week.

He'd made 11 calls, before Amkey. They weren't cold calls. Some were repeats, others were leads, people who were potential customers. If not ready to buy, they were at least thinking about buying. He'd closed two sales (before Amkey) and each was for multiple products. That wasn't bad, sales-wise or commission-wise.

But the other calls, which took up the lion's share of Charlie's time that week, what were they like?

They were mostly negative. He heard about his competition, how terrific they were, what swell features their products had, how easy they were to do business with. He heard about his products and their shortcomings. He heard about his prices, and their height. He heard this kind of thing over and over.

And even the buyers who placed orders hit Charlie with negative comments. Remember? One said he was sure he could do better, but couldn't take time to shop around. The other said he picked Charlie's firm only because they could meet his delivery schedule.

By Friday afternoon, Charlie's job had really done a job on him. He went into the Amkey negotiation almost powerless because he saw himself that way. He went in thinking he had all the pressures and all the problems, and the buyer had none.

He went in thinking he'd probably lost the sale and his one slim chance of getting it would be to cut the price . . . again. He entered the negotiation not ready to negotiate but ready to cave in. And that's exactly what he did.

The fact of the matter was that Charlie *had* the Amkey order before he walked through the door that Friday. They were going to see if they could nudge the price a little, because that was their job. But they regarded the price in the proposal as a pretty good one, and were fully prepared to go with it. For a number of reasons.

1. Amkey could get comparable prices for comparable products from one or two of Charlie's competitors, but couldn't get the terms they needed anywhere else. Terms were important to them.
2. Amkey didn't need the features the competitors had that Charlie didn't have. But they did need one feature he had that his competitors lacked.
3. The Amkey manager and buyer appreciated the fact that Charlie had worked for the order; had brought his support people in to study the work-

flow, in a sensible, logical way. They liked the general solution in the proposal; they saw the long-
range savings they'd realize.
4. Amkey had looked into Charlie's company and
   learned that it *does* stand behind its products and
   does service them promptly. They didn't want to
   have to worry about maintenance.
5. They liked Charlie. They'd seen him only three
   times before that Friday, but they regarded him as
   a straightforward, conscientious guy. They looked
   forward to doing business with him.

Charlie had all these things going for him before he
went into that Amkey negotiation—and not even the *possibility* of any of them ever occurred to him. Can you blame
him?

He went into that room virtually powerless because he
thought he was, thought his only weapon was to cut the
price even further. But that was all in his head. His job
had put it there.

A friend of mine once put it aptly. He said:

"We call ourselves salesmen. But in a way, that's wrong.
We spend most of our time *not* making the sale. We spend
most of our time listening to people tell us why they're *not*
buying. We spend only some of our time making the sale.
Sounds funny, but when you think about it, we get a lot
more practice *not* making the sale than we do selling."

Well, he said it. Your job conditions you to go into negotiation in a negative frame of mind. Your job, most of the
time, brings you criticism and complaints—about your
products, your prices—and compliments, about your competitors. Your job brainwashes you. You hear these things
often enough and you begin to believe them. And if you
don't call a halt to this kind of thinking, you're sunk.

But you can change it, easily. You can shift your mental gears. You can do it because power is in the eyes of the beholder. It's been proven time and time again. Power is a state of mind. You have as much as you think you have.

I'll show you.

2

Power Is What You Think It Is

As we saw, Charlie left his Amkey negotiation a happy man. He'd have to deal with his boss, and the pricing guy at the home office. But he had closed the sale. That, in his mind, was the important thing. But, in a sense, Charlie's bliss was based on ignorance.

The price in his proposal to Amkey, already discounted, was $78,000. When he so quickly cut it another nine percent—without being asked, mind you—he reduced it by another $7020. He didn't have to make that price cut. By making it, he left $7020 on the table. And it was $7020 pure profit.

If Charlie had been more quiet and more patient at Amkey, if he had listened, perhaps probed, he would have learned he was not sitting at that table without power. He wouldn't have left the seven grand on the table. He would have left the deal happier, the customer would have been just as happy, his boss would have been happy, and his company would have made that much more profit.

How much have you left on the table in your sales career? Ten thousand dollars? A hundred thousand dollars? A million dollars? Depending on what you sell, and how long you've been selling it, you could have left behind any one of these totals, or any number in between. They were dollars that were there for the asking—for the taking. And the dollars were all profit.

When we close a sale, we usually leave the deal happy, whatever the terms. After all, the idea is—to make the sale. But now and then we learn that we'd settled for 80 cents when we could have easily gotten 85 cents, or for $30, when we could have gotten $35, or for $300,000—when all we had to do was hold out a little longer and we would have gotten $350,000.

It's happened to all of us, dozens of times.

Why didn't we get that extra nickel, or that extra five dollars, or that extra fifty grand? Simple. Because, like Charlie, we underestimated our own power and overestimated the power of the buyer.

We were convinced the buyer was holding 51 cards and we had one—the discount—and even that was a kind of a joker because we had to argue with the home office for the discount authority.

Charlie had all kinds of things going for him when he walked through the Amkey door that Friday afternoon. They liked him. They liked his product. They liked his company's reputation for service. They couldn't get their terms from his competitors. They appreciated the thoroughness of his proposal. They were ready to go with the discount in the proposal.

It never occurred to Charlie that any one of these things was even possible.

Every one was a source of power for Charlie.

And there could have been even more. Maybe the buyers were out of time; they wanted to close the deal that day and move on to something else. Maybe an important vice president with a technical background had mildly expressed a preference for Charlie's product. That would have made him virtually a sole source vendor. Maybe Charlie was the only vendor who could deliver fast enough for the buyer. That gave him an edge.

Recall the customer who told Charlie he got the order because he could meet the delivery schedule? Charlie viewed that comment negatively, but he shouldn't have. An efficient delivery system was his source of power in that negotiation.

Power is a funny thing. It's what we think it is. That doesn't mean it isn't real. It's very real, and a source of enormous strength in negotiating. But it's largely in our minds. It is as strong, or as weak, as we believe it is.

Seeing is believing. If we *see* the sources of power, and *believe* they are sources of power, then they are. And if we don't see them, they might as well not be there.

Charlie didn't see any of his powers in that negotiation, and look at what happened to him. If he'd seen just a couple or maybe even one of the things he had going for him, he wouldn't have left that $7020 on the table. If he'd just *considered the possibility* that any of those conditions were present, he wouldn't have been so quick to cut his price again.

Charlie couldn't have read the buyers' minds. We all know that.

But he could have been far less preoccupied with his own problems and pressures. He could have given more thought to the possible problems and pressures confronting the buyer. He could have been more concerned with making a better deal—being a better negotiator. And if he had thought along these lines, he would have behaved differently.

He would have been more patient. He would have taken more time, and turned time to his advantage. He wouldn't have been so anxious to price-cut. He would have asked questions. He would have listened, and listened. He would also have talked—about his product, about his company, about his service, about the economy or the weather . . . about everything but price.

Even before his meetings with the buyers (there were three, remember) he would have struck up friendly idle conversations with other employees. In short, he would have done a variety of things to help him pick up information, to help him discover facts or opinions or conditions that could be, for him, sources of power in negotiation. He would have taken *time*. And in negotiation *time is money*.

In the course of the most idle conversation, information can fall out—information that provides clues to facts or conditions that in some way limit the buyer's power—and increase the seller's power. Maybe the engineering department is screaming at the buyer to hurry up with the acquisition of that component they need, and they don't care whether it costs $5 or $6. Maybe the buyer has 50 other requisitions under that one and simply has no time to bargain. Remember the customer who told Charlie he was sure he could have done better, but didn't have time to shop around? That was Charlie's source of power in that one.

For the sales person, negotiation is a process of discovery—a process during which he discovers his possible sources of power.

Once he uncovers his sources of power, the sales person then must decide the most effective way to use them.

Power is strange. Not only do people view it differently, they use it differently. On occasion, even, they see it but fail to use it at all.

Dr. Chester L. Karrass, whose research we mentioned earlier, was interested in what he called the "paradox of power." He asked this question: Why will one negotiator with very little power go to the table showing enormous strength and vigor while another negotiator with a great deal of power will enter a negotiation meek and intimidated?

What Dr. Karrass found, in short, is that power is what you think it is. Those who think they have no power negotiate poorly and weakly—even if they *do* have power. Those who think they have power negotiate from strength —even if they *don't* really have the power.

Power is largely a state of mind. We've seen how our salesman, Charlie Miller, left a large amount of money on the table because he went in feeling powerless. There was no power in his head. Even though, as we have seen, he had many sources of power working for him—if he had thought about them, thought about even the possibility that they existed.

The power you bring to your negotiations in the future will depend largely on your frame of mind. But your sources of power are very real. We're going into them now, one by one.

3

The Power Your Competition Gives You

As sales people, we live with our competition. We sell with the competition in mind, we negotiate thinking about the competition. If we forget about the competitors over the weekend, the first buyer we see on Monday morning reminds us of them.

The main reason we lower our prices is—the competition. And, of course, buyers know this.

The fact is, your competition can be a source of power to you in negotiation—and often is. Outlandish? Hardly. There are limits to the buyer's ability to use your competition, reasons he cannot or will not buy from them. And, in this sense, competition works for you. Competition helps you close the order.

Have buyers said something like this to you? "A computer is a computer is a computer, just give me your best price." Or, "A chemical is a chemical is a chemical, what's the lowest price?" Or, "A dye is a dye is a dye, they're all the same to me. I need the lowest price."

Of course. Substitute your product and you've heard that kind of thing, many times over. Why?

The buyer knows that if you believe that you and your competitors are all the same to him, that your products are the same, that your service is the same, you will assume you have only one way to be different: by lowering the price.

That's the buyer's job—to get the product he wants at a lower price. And he knows that if you're convinced that's the only way you can make the sale, you'll do your best to lower it.

But *are* you and your competitors all the same to the buyer? Let's say you have ten competitors. Can the buyer pick up the phone and get what he wants from any of the ten? Or, will he?

The answer is no. Or very, very rarely.

There may be ten companies that could supply a service or a part for General Electric. But can GE buy from any of the ten? Aren't there limits on the buyer's ability to use the competition?

Here's one kind of limit. The head of data processing for a Fortune 500 company attended my negotiation seminar not long ago. He recalled that when he first started out in that business 20 years ago he recommended the purchase of a new system from one of the larger computer companies.

The machine never worked right; it was one problem after another. And, what was more, the seller never really conscientiously tried to straighten out the trouble.

"This week I have to get a quote from this company, for

a $5 million system," he said. "But I still resent what happened 20 years ago and I'll find some valid reason, some justification, for buying from someone else."

Wasn't that old bad experience with that company, which he'll never forget, a limit on his ability to use the competition? Of course. But the other sellers bidding on the new system won't assume a major competitor doesn't stand a chance.

Here's another kind of limit. We book hotel space for our seminars. Usually, when we call, some hotels simply don't have the space we need when we need it. Isn't that a limit on my ability to use the competition? When I'm talking to the seller at the hotel that does have space, he assumes I can get the space anywhere. He's thinking of all the competition. But the fact is I usually can't. That restricts my use of the competition.

Another example, about terms. Our accounting system pays in 30 days. Some hotels want cash in advance. Our accounting system can't handle the cash-in-advance kind of payment. So that limits my ability to use some of the competition. But the hotel sales people who do give me 30 days probably figure all other hotels do too. They don't realize that I can only use those certain hotels that will give us the terms we need.

What about the capacity to produce and deliver? Do all your competitors have your company's ability to produce in quantity, the ability to deliver on time?

Some companies go in with terrific prices—but they can't deliver the goods.

Remember the old story about the butcher?

The customer goes into the butcher shop and asks, "How much is filet mignon?"

"Five dollars a pound," the butcher says.

The customer replies, "But Henry across the street sells it for $4.50 a pound."

"Well, you'll have to get it there, then."

The customer explained, "He doesn't have any."

The butcher answered, "If I didn't have any, you could have it for $4 a pound."

It's easy enough for a sales person to go in with a low price—if he can't fill or deliver the order anyway.

The butcher's customer couldn't go to the competition simply because he didn't have the product.

Here's another limit to my ability to use competition.

We order large quantities of audio tapes, part of the material used in seminars. Recently I asked four outfits to bid. Three of them didn't even show up. The guy who showed up got the order.

The salesman who came didn't know the others had not responded. He came by my office at eleven o'clock. What was going on in his mind? Probably he was thinking the other three had been there before ten o'clock, and he negotiated with that in mind.

My ability to use the competition was certainly limited in that case.

Are there still other kinds of limits to my use of the competition?

Imagine for a moment that I'm a buyer of your product. I'm thinking about you and your ten competitors, all the companies I, theoretically, could buy your particular product from.

One of your competitors got me in trouble once. The thing was late, it didn't work right, the engineering people were mad. Doing business with that company hurt my career. Am I going to consider them again? Not likely. But other sellers don't know that, and regard that firm as a competitor, and negotiate from that standpoint.

Another one of your competitors is just too far away. Prices are okay, but dealing with them is cumbersome and time-consuming. Too much trouble.

Still another one of your competitors doesn't have a good reputation. I've talked with other buyers in my industry and this company doesn't have a good track record. Am I going to chance that?

There's another company in your business that won't give me 90 days credit, and I need that. And another that just doesn't deliver on time. I need dependable delivery.

There are all sorts of things that limit my ability as a buyer to use the competition.

Some sources don't offer the full line of service that I require. Some sources are just too expensive. Others don't have a good warranty—or one that looks good on paper but isn't reliable. In one case, I don't like the salesman—or the way he talks, or the way he dresses.

Maybe I have a longterm relationship with you and your company. I like you and I like your company and I like doing business with you. It's fast and easy. Won't that limit my use of the competition—even if their prices are a little lower?

Say your product and those of two other companies were qualified by the engineers for the order. The head of engineering tells me, the buyer, which three qualified. But then he also says he liked yours best—it worked best, it looked like it would give them the least trouble. Am I going to buy one of the other two? Even if yours is more expensive, I'll figure out a way to justify the additional cost.

Sometimes the buyer's ability to use the competition is limited by built-in specification designs that explicitly or implicitly exclude some of the competition, or put them at a disadvantage in bidding.

A friend of mine was interested in building a new swimming pool. One of the pool salesmen convinced him that a certain kind of filter system was best. "Buy any pool you want, but be sure to get that kind of filter," the sales person told my friend.

The other pool companies bidding on the job could get the kind of filter my friend wanted. But they didn't regularly use that kind, and would have to go buy it. The firm of the salesman who made the recommendation consistently used that filter, bought them by the hundreds. So they were in an advantageous position—they could come in with a lower bid, without sacrificing profit.

The buyer's use of the competition can be limited because the end user in his organization *thinks* your product is better—even if it isn't.

A buyer friend of mine bought the same kind of paint for his maintenance people for some years. Then he found another brand that sold for 30 percent less. He had it analyzed, and it proved to be exactly the same as the paint he had been buying. He ordered some.

Immediately after trying the new brand paint for the first time, the maintenance people called the buyer. "It doesn't go on right," they complained.

The buyer explained the paint was identical, explained the analysis he had had done. The maintenance people just repeated, "It doesn't go on right."

To prove a point to himself, the buyer went to the maintenance department in the middle of the night and poured the new brand paint in the cans of the old brand.

"Goes on great," the maintenance people reported the next morning.

The end user in that organization thought a product was better even though it wasn't. Didn't that limit the buyer's ability to use the competition?

My friend wasn't going to spend his nights swapping paint and paint cans, so he went back to the old brand— the more expensive one.

You yourself can limit my ability to use the competition. Maybe I like your manner, your conscientiousness, your personality. We get along well. It's a pleasure doing business with you. Doesn't that work against my use of the competition?

A summary thought on competition: the buyer will always want to buy the most reliable product from the company with the best reputation—but at the price of the most unreliable product from the most unreliable seller.

Suppose you represent a highly reputable company that markets good printers for computing systems, services them well, and has for years. A new little outfit opens up shop in a garage—a new competitor, with low overhead and low prices.

The buyer will want your product at the low price of the garage-headquartered company. He may even tell you in glowing terms about the new outfit and its low prices. But will he buy from them? Will he take that risk? Would you? Probably not.

To say that buyers always make their decisions based

on price is like saying everyone marries for money. Few do. Most don't.

There's another way competition can be a source of power for you. That is, if the buyer thinks he is in competition with others for your product, your time. And it happens. I'll give you a personal example.

I wanted to rent a three-quarter-inch video player. I called a video supply house—ready to negotiate.

"Do you have three-quarter-inch players to rent?" I asked.

"Yes," the seller replied.

"How much are they?"

"A hundred dollars a day. But hold on." Then he called to a fellow employee, "Hey George, do we have any three-quarter-inch players left?" The voice came back, "Yes. One."

Now, how good a deal do you think I made after that? I paid the hundred dollars.

If the buyer feels in competition for your product, he is much less likely to worry about price.

Remember the Susan B. Anthony dollars? The government had trouble getting rid of them. But at one place, the post office in San Francisco, people lined up to buy them. Why? They had put up a sign that said: SUSAN B. ANTHONY DOLLARS. LIMIT TWO TO A CUSTOMER. People felt in competition for the product.

Let's say the buyer's heard that other companies in his industry are buying your product, and having very good experience with it. He's heard your company is doing better all the time, getting a larger share of the market all the time. And, from what he's heard, your company deserves it.

He comes to you. He comes to you feeling he's competing for you. And he's not in a very good bargaining position.

He's in competition with other customers for your product, and that's a source of power to you.

4

The Power of Commitment

Commitment is one of the strongest powers you have going for you in negotiation. The trick is—knowing how to use it.

There are four kinds of commitment that strengthen your position at the bargaining table:

1. Commitment to your own organization
2. Commitment on the part of persons in the buyer organization
3. Person-to-person commitment
4. Commitment to your own targets and goals

Let's take them one by one.

Commitment to your own organization means commitment to your company, its people, its products, and its services. You can't fake this. You must be sincerely convinced of the merit of your organization and what it does, and you must constantly fortify that conviction.

If you have that conviction, and keep it strong, it can be a powerful ally in negotiation. Its benefits will take the shape of more closings and more profitable closings.

An incident that shows how this commitment can work for you occurred not long ago when I visited an old friend, now marketing vice president for a large firm that sells process control systems.

I was talking with my friend, whose name is Sam, in his office when his secretary buzzed his phone. He talked to her for a minute, then turned to me. "Excuse me, Gary. I have to see a district manager. It'll only take a few minutes." I volunteered to leave, to wait in the outer office, but he suggested I stay. I moved to a chair in the corner of the room and began leafing through a magazine.

The district manager came in, he and Sam shook hands, and Sam introduced me briefly as an old friend. Then Sam and the district manager, whose name was Hank, sat down across from each other at the desk.

Sam spoke first. "Now, what can I do for you, Hank?"

"It's the Lonergan company proposal, Sam. We can get that business. And it's good business. But we've got to figure how to shave the price some more."

Sam was silent for a moment. Then: "I remember the proposal, Hank. It was a good one. But didn't we already knock the price down from the original one?"

"Well, we took it down ten percent. But that won't do it, Sam. The buyer says the competition is low-balling us all over the company. If you can give me another ten percent, even nine percent, I think we can nail it down. It's a big order, Sam, and that company's growing all the time."

Sam looked at the district manager for a few seconds.

Then he leaned across his desk. "Hank, you've been with the company for what, thirteen, fifteen years?"

"Fifteen, this October."

"You think it's a pretty good company?"

"The best in the business, Sam. Best in the country, probably."

"You think we're an honorable company, an honest company?"

"Of course. We bend over backward to be squeaky clean. Always have."

"Some of our competitors pull shoddy stunts, Hank. You know that. What happens if one of our guys does something like that?"

"He gets canned."

"And we let one go every now and then, don't we, Hank? Fire him right on the spot."

"We sure do."

"But that kind of thing doesn't come up very often, does it, Hank? Why?"

"We hire good people, the best we can find."

"And we do our best to keep them—pay them well, recognize accomplishment, give them good benefits. Isn't that true?"

"Sure."

"What about our products, Hank? You think our systems are pretty good?"

"Better than 90 percent of what's out there. As good as the other ten percent."

"And our prices—how do they stack up?"

"Sometimes we're a little high going in. Some of our competitors really get their numbers down. But in the long run we're the best buy. Always have been."

"And our service—is that okay?"

"Nobody stands behind their stuff the way we do. We're known for that. We back up our systems all the way. Remember that glitch at the appliance company? The two guys who knew that problem backward and forward were in New York, and you brought them back to go in there and get it straightened out."

"We sure did. And it costs money to do that. But we did it because that's the way we do business." Sam leaned back in his chair. "Hank, you've sat here and told me we have the best company, we have good people and we take care of them, the best service, products at the top of the heap, prices that are a little high but a long-term cost that is low; that we're a good investment for the customer.

"Your proposal to Lonergan was a good one, a thorough one, and I'm sure they know that. The original price you quoted was a fair one—fair to the customers and fair to us. Since then, you lowered it ten percent. Well, that's all right.

"Now you want to drop it another ten percent, or nine percent. You say the buyer wants more discount. Well, that's the buyer's job—you know that, he's doing his job. Good for him. But does that mean he'll walk away if we don't respond to that nudge? We don't really know his answer to that, do we?

"Now, Hank, I want to ask you this: If you owned this company, if you hired the best people, turned out the best product you could, serviced it in a superior fashion, invested heavily in research and development, did business as honestly as you knew how, what would you want your people to do?

"Would you want them to get the prices that the products and the company deserve? Would you want them to have confidence in their organization, their prices? Or would you want them to get down to the level of some of our competitors, like that new outfit in Houston whose systems fall apart in six months, or like those who price-cut, deliver the systems, take the money and run? You know that game, Hank. We've both picked up the pieces of those kinds of deals dozens of times, bailed customers out dozens of times.

"What would you want, if you owned this company?"

Sam's district manager stood up and walked to a large window at the other side of the office. "I don't know, Sam," he said. "I know what you say is true. Still—another nine or ten percent and I think we can get the order."

"If we cut the price another 50 percent, we'd get plenty of orders," Sam said. "We'd be very busy—as we went out of business."

Hank stared out of the window silently for a few moments. Then: "Maybe you're right, Sam. I worked hard on that proposal. It's exactly what they need. Nobody can do better for them. And we have already dropped it ten percent. Yes. You're right. We don't want to get in a price war with some of those outfits—competitors who don't offer half the reliability we do. I'll go back. We'll go in again. We'll talk more. We'll hold tight. And well, we'll see."

They shook hands and Hank headed for the door. "It was good seeing you," Sam said after him. Hank closed the door behind him and Sam turned to me.

"I know the management books say you shouldn't go through something like that with an employee when there's another person present. But I wanted you to hear it.

"I go through that kind of thing every day, at least a couple of times. It's a constant struggle. I don't blame these guys. I was out there long enough and I know how it is. The customers hammer at your prices, give you static about the competitors. It gets to you after a while. You have to constantly fight what you're hearing, what's going on in your own mind. But I did it. And guys like Hank have to do it, too. They have to remember. The point is, if they think the product's worth the price—they get it.

"I was a good salesman, a good branch manager, and a good district manager. That's why I'm here now. I was good because I kept myself convinced that we have the best deal for the customer, and we do: products, service, reliability. We're always a little high on price. But our reputation more than justifies it. Buy our system and we're mother hen to it for the rest of its life. That's worth a lot.

"More and more, the customer's business depends on our systems. They foul up, the customer can lose his shirt. We worry about that. A lot of our competitors don't. I don't even know how you put a price on that attitude.

"Hank's one of the best guys out there. He's as committed to the company as I am. But he wants to make the sale. He doesn't want to lose the sale. He let his commitment slip his mind for a while. It's my job to bring his commitment back. If they believe the company is good, they get the price."

Sam's career in business, and it's a brilliant one, was built on this commitment. It was his principal source of power all the way up the line to the vice presidency he now holds. And it still is. His company's reputation, and it's a good one, is based on commitment.

Commitment to his organization is one of the strongest sources of power that a sales person has going for him. The stronger his belief—in his company, its products, its practices—the more confident he is, the better negotiator he is.

Charlie Miller's company had good products, a good reputation for service and for favorable terms. He knew this as well as anyone. But he didn't give these things a thought when he sat there waiting for his appointment at Amkey. It "slipped his mind for a while." Nothing but dollar signs ran around in his head. They were his prices, and the more he thought about them, the higher they seemed to him. So he ended up leaving a good deal of money on the table.

Remember when Charlie first got back from his sales meeting? He felt a good deal of commitment to his organization that first day. He was confident in his company, its products, its plans. But as the days wore on, as he went through his job, his commitment waned, his confidence waned. He didn't keep his defenses up. He didn't fight what he was hearing, he didn't fight what was going on in his own mind. He let the power of commitment to his organization slip from his grasp.

When a sales person feels the kind of commitment that my friend Sam feels, it shows. Pride in his company and its output, loyalty to his company—these contribute to his confidence, his success in negotiation.

Now for the second kind of commitment on our list: *commitment on the part of persons in the buyer organization.*

A young sales woman I know is especially adept at gathering this kind of commitment. She spends a great deal of time at the companies she sells to, and not just with buyers. She drops in on engineers, technicians—the end users of her product. She strikes up conversations with them. She elicits their opinions about her products and, on occasion, is privy to their opinions about her competitors' products.

She gathers expressions of satisfaction about her products. She gathers commitment. Once these people have voiced their positive opinions, they will stand behind them, because they're standing behind their own words.

And they will defend them. They will not back off.

Sometimes she even gets their commitment in writing, by way of arranging advertising or publicity for them— endorsing her products and explaining how they use them to their advantage, how they benefit from them.

Do you think this commitment—on the part of people within her buyer organizations—is a source of power to her in negotiation? You can bet it is.

Our third kind of commitment that is a source of power is *person-to-person commitment.*

Put another way, this is the power of the personal relationship. Or put still another way, it is the power of commitment to the satisfaction of someone else—the buyer.

On the surface it appears that the person-to-person commitment, the power of the personal relationship, is something that is a long time developing. And it may be. The seller and the buyer get to like and respect each other, have a drink together after work, maybe play golf. They become personal friends, each committed to playing fair with the other. And that's fine.

But you can show the buyer from the very outset of a relationship that you are committed to his satisfaction—

and build the personal relationship by demonstrating that commitment.

Maybe you never have a drink together or play golf together, but you can still build a strong personal business relationship through this commitment. It becomes a second relationship. There is the relationship of your company to his company and there is the relationship of you to him—as individuals, as one business person to another.

You say to him, in effect, "You buy these systems from me and you will not be hurt. *I* (as an individual) will make sure you are satisfied. *I* will make sure they do what they are supposed to do. *I* will make sure my company properly supports the systems. If something does go wrong, *I* will make sure it is corrected and corrected promptly. You will not have to worry about delivery, you will not have to worry about installation, you will not have to worry about performance. *I* will take care of these things. *I* will protect you."

Now of course you must really feel your commitment as an individual to the buyer as an individual—and do what you say you will do. If you do, it can lead to a degree of trust, trust in you on the buyer's part, that is beyond measure in importance.

Use this power to reduce the buyer's concerns and worries, to give him security, and he will think less about whether the price is $3 or $3.50, or $3000 or $3500. You have made him feel nice and safe doing business with you. That is important to him. That has a value to him.

The fourth commitment on our list is the *commitment to your own targets and goals*. This is, in a sense, commitment to yourself, and your word.

If you *really* commit to yourself that you will make a

certain number of sales, and not go below a certain price, it's probable you will live up to that commitment. If you go a step further, and make the same commitment to your boss, it's even more highly probable that you will live up to it.

Why? Because you'll suffer a loss of ego if you don't. And because of this, we tend to do those things we really commit to do—commit to ourselves and to others.

There was an interesting experiment done with two groups of chemical sales people.

One group was told the starting price was $1 a pound, the target was 98 cents a pound and the very least they could take was 96 cents. Most orders came in at 96 cents.

Another group was told the starting price was $1 a pound, the target was 98 cents, and the minimum was 95 cents. Most orders came in at 95 cents.

The 96 cents and the 95 cents were commitments— kinds of forced commitments. Nonetheless, in each case the sales people were committed not to go below a certain price. And they didn't.

You can make that kind of commitment to yourself, the commitment not only to make more deals, but better deals. The more specific, the better: you will sell this many units and never go below this price. You can write it down and put it in your pocket and take it out and look at it now and then as a reminder. Or, as we said, you can tell your boss, or write it down for him.

If you *make* the commitment seriously, and *take* it seriously, you will stick to it. But it has to be *your* commitment.

There's a piece of advice here for sales management people. Don't tell the sales people how many units they must sell and what price they must get. If you do, it takes the form of *your* commitment. And it may or may not become *their* commitment.

Sit down with the sales people individually. You and they come to common agreement on how many units and on what price. Then it is their commitment as well as yours. And the chances of their adhering to it are much greater.

Some of the great marketing organizations in industry were built on the principle of commitment. Develop and constantly fortify that commitment—to your organization, to yourself, to your customers—and you will be stronger, and more successful, in every negotiation.

5

The Power of Wooing

Recently I was in Palm Springs to make a speech and went to a highly recommended restaurant for dinner. There was a line of customers waiting for tables.

Like most people, I don't like lines. I resent them. But I thought, gee, the place must be really good. And I got in line.

I was surprised when the hostess approached me. "I'm sorry about the line," she said. "It will be about 15 minutes. We appreciate your waiting. Can I bring you a chair, or a complimentary cup of coffee?"

After that, I didn't mind waiting in the line for a few minutes. She had wooed me, successfully.

The owner of that restaurant had learned that, even when business is very good, it's smart to woo the customer just as you do when business is bad, or when there is no business at all.

The hostess made me feel they really wanted my business. They certainly didn't need it, but they wanted it.

We sellers often confuse *want* and *need*. Certainly we don't want to give the buyer the idea we're desperate, that we'll go out of business if we don't get his order. But we do want to make it clear we want his order, that we want to do business with him.

Sales people who work for large companies with large shares of the market, with products much in demand, or sales people who are sole sources for certain products, often forget to woo the customer. And wooing is especially important in this kind of situation.

Not long ago I went with a friend who wanted to look at models of an expensive German import car. He was genuinely interested; he looked over the cars carefully, and liked one in particular.

He asked the salesman, "How much do you think I can get out with, on this model?"

The salesman replied, "Pardon me?"

My friend repeated his question. "How much do you think I can get out with—what kind of price can I get?"

The salesman replied, "About $45,000."

My friend was taken aback. "That's higher than the price on the tag."

The salesman replied, "Well, there's tax and license."

My friend tried again. "What I meant was—what price do you think I could figure on—out the door?"

"Oh," the salesman replied. "*We* don't negotiate. There's superb engineering in these cars. They sell well. We don't come down in price. We never come down. They sell."

My friend was an intelligent man and asked questions to test price.

How did my friend feel? He felt, of course, that they

not only didn't need his business, but didn't want it either. His reaction was, screw them. If they don't need me, I sure as hell don't need them. For $45,000 there's a lot of other cars around.

How could that sales person have handled the situation differently? And perhaps even have made the sale, even though he couldn't lower the price?

He could have said something like this:

"I'd like you to have this car, and I'd certainly like to make the sale. And I'll go in to the manager with any offer you want to make.

"But I can tell you honestly, they've never taken an offer yet. They never come down on price. It's not the dealership here. They set the prices in Germany. But people keep buying them and they keep appreciating.

"I used to work at another dealership for another kind of car and they negotiated offers. But here, they just don't come down. Customers have very good experience with the cars, and they hold their value extremely well. But listen, I really want to make this sale so I'll try whatever you like."

If the salesman had taken this approach, my friend may have left trying to figure out how he'd raise the money to buy the car. Instead, he left feeling offended.

Part of the power of wooing is the power of work. Imagine for a minute that you needed new equipment for your word processing department, and asked a couple of companies to make proposals.

The first company was the ranking name in the field, the one with much of the business and a good reputation. The second was a smaller firm, much smaller, but also known to be reliable.

Three sales people in three-button suits make a well-rehearsed standard proposal for your business. They are knowledgeable, polite, but also impersonal and aloof. They give you the impression they're not open to negotiating because they're so big, and so successful. And they are. They finish their proposal, and their spokesman tells you they will give you time to think about it and call you the following week.

A lone representative comes from the smaller company. He asks a lot of questions about your company and your word processing operation and needs. He's genuinely interested in your problems, and in your business. He goes away and comes back two days later with a tailored proposal, one that shows a great deal of work. He goes over it, shows how the equipment he's proposing is especially suited to your particular department, and its growth pattern.

"We think we can really help you with our equipment," he says. "We think we can help that department go better, and grow better. We'd certainly like to have your business. It would be good for us, and especially good for you. And we believe you'll be well satisfied."

Would you have a difficult time not giving the order to the first group of sales people? Not at all. As a matter of fact, you may well enjoy it—get a feeling you've beat the system.

But wouldn't you have a hard time (on a personal level) telling the other salesman he didn't get the order after he did so much work? Certainly you would. He wooed you. He wooed you because he worked hard to get your business and because he wanted your business. You felt your business would be important to him.

There is power in persistently wanting the business. Not *needing* it, but *wanting* it.

At our company, we gave all of our printing business to one firm for about five years. It was convenient to do it that way; changing is a nuisance.

But a sales person from another printing company paid calls on us every week—month after month. Each time he had new samples of his company's work to show us. Each time he made it clear how much he wanted at least part of our printing business. And eventually he got it.

We've all hired employees. We look over their backgrounds, their credentials. We interview them. But what's the thing that impresses us most? How much they want the job. If we have several applicants who are qualified, we lean toward the one who gives us the impression he or she really wants that job, can't wait to get going, can't wait to do, and to learn.

Sometimes we may even choose an applicant who is not quite as well qualified in terms of training or experience as others but who demonstrates by attitude how much he wants to do the work—and learn to do it better.

If the applicant leaves us with the impression he's desperately in need of work, we back off. We look to the other people applying.

But needing is far different than wanting. It wouldn't hurt if every one of us in sales told ourselves each morning: I don't need, but I *want*, the business.

6

The Power of Taking Risks

In our negotiation seminars we start off our discussion of risk this way:

I hold a quarter in my hand. I say to the group, "I want to make a bet with you. I'll flip this quarter. If it comes out heads, I owe you a million dollars. If it comes out tails, you owe me $100,000.

"We must make two assumptions. One is that if you lose, you can borrow the money from the bank. If I lose, I can get the money from the bank.

"Again: heads, you're a millionaire. Tails, you owe me $100,000. How many would take the bet?"

Is that a good bet? It certainly is. Your chance of winning a million dollars is the same as your chance of losing one-tenth of that.

But usually only a few people in the group will raise their hands, indicating their willingness to take such a bet.

Why? Because most are afraid of the risk involved. They're viewing it from the standpoint of the loss.

If I tell the group they can chip in to make the bet with me—that is, they can syndicate the bet among themselves—then a great many more raise their hands. Why? Because that way they're reducing the risk, sharing the loss, if it occurs.

But, of course, they're also reducing their winnings, as individuals. None becomes a millionaire. The more you're willing to risk, the more you can gain; the less you're willing to risk, the less you can win.

Does risk play a part in negotiation? It sure does. A very important part. Francis Bacon said, "All negotiation is to look, discover, and take risks." If you and I are negotiating and your willingness to take risks is greater than mine, you have an edge—regardless of the other factors involved.

If I'm a buyer there are risks I don't want to take, especially if I'm in a large organization. Am I going to switch from your product to another, less familiar to me, just because it is a little cheaper? Am I going to jeopardize an important project—or jeopardize my job?

Some projects, especially in large organizations, represent very high investment—in planning, in design, in engineering. And the cost of a mistake can be very high.

If I can get the quality I want and the reliability I want from your company, won't I pay a little more for that? Will I take a chance and switch to another company to save five or ten percent if the switch represents a risk? Won't I be willing to pay a premium if it means I won't have to worry about a mistake—a mistake that could jam an important project, or close down a manufacturing line?

You can bet I will, if I value my career, my job. I can always find a way to justify paying a little more.

This is especially true if I'm a buyer for a large, bureaucratic company. I'm not encouraged to take chances—there's too much at stake. And I have higher-ups looking over my shoulder, Monday morning quarterbacks.

I'll negotiate and I'll negotiate as skillfully as I can. I'll tell you I can buy what I need from many sources; I'll leave you with the impression there's no risk involved. But I'll negotiate carefully. I'll avoid taking risks.

Does this give you an advantage? Certainly. It means you can hold the line longer on your prices. It means you can risk a little more. And make a better deal.

My unwillingness to risk is a source of power to you, the seller. And if I appear to have forgotten the risks involved in going to another company, you can remind me. Subtly.

At our office, we were looking into new copying machines. One sales person demonstrated his, then said this:

"We've tracked our frequency of repair record very carefully. We've tracked it in our own plant and in customer locations. It's improved steadily, month after month, as we've enhanced our machines. We're convinced it's the best in the industry.

"Whatever machine you consider, look into its repair record. We don't believe there's any that compare with ours.

"Also, be sure to ask about service. We stand behind our equipment. We respond quickly when you need us. So be careful—there are a lot of new outfits in the business. They deliver the machine, collect their bill, and you never see them again."

That salesman didn't slander any particular competitors. He talked about the pitfalls of purchasing in his market, and did it in a way that seemed like he was helping me, educating me, to deal more efficiently with sales people of his industry.

While he was saying these things, what was I thinking? I was wondering about the frequency of repair record of other companies in that business. I was worrying about the possibility of buying a machine that would break down a lot—from a company that wouldn't support its products.

I was wondering, in sum, if it would be riskier to buy from someone else than from him. He had successfully reminded me of the element of risk.

There are always risks in buying. There's the risk the seller can't meet the production rate the buyer needs. There's the risk the company might not deliver on time. There's the risk the product won't work, or will work for awhile, then stop. There's the risk of the supplier's failure to back up his product. There's the risk of improper billing.

It's the sales person's job to point out the reduced risk of dealing with him and, gracefully, the increased risk in dealing with his competitors.

Sometimes the seller has to deal with risks that are in the buyer's mind but don't really exist. But if the buyer perceives a risk, to him it *is* a risk, and the sales person must alleviate his concern.

In this kind of situation the concept of the moneyback guarantee is useful.

One of the cardinal rules of the mail order business is: Always offer the customer a moneyback guarantee. Why do they do this? It reduces the risk of buying.

If my attention is attracted by an ad for a product in the back of some magazine, I'm probably interested in that product. Chances are I've never done business with the company selling it, probably never even heard of the company.

I can't see the product to look it over before I buy. I must go on the printed description and perhaps an illustration. I see all kinds of risks: the thing may not be what it looks like; it may not be what they say it is; it may not do what they say it will do.

But then I notice that the ad says this: "If you are not fully satisfied with the product, return it and we will refund your money."

The risks I envisioned disappear. What's to worry about? If I don't like it, I'll send it back and get a refund. What have I got to lose?

Sears built its reputation on the slogan, "Satisfaction guaranteed."

I know a printer who always delivers on time. It's a matter of principle with him—to deliver the job when he said he'd deliver it.

But a lot of printers don't deliver on time. They invariably run a day or two late, or a week late.

When a new customer goes to my printer friend, that customer has no way of knowing that he does, indeed, always deliver on time. He's heard those kinds of promises from printers before. He sees a risk of late delivery, one that, in this case, doesn't exist.

How does this printer deal with this?

When he realizes that his new customer is concerned about delivery time, he introduces the customer to his production manager, and his plant manager. While the customer is there, they all agree on the delivery date.

Then the printer puts the delivery date in writing, makes the commitment in writing. He has even gone so far as to say, "If we don't deliver on time, you don't have to pay." This is, in effect, a kind of guarantee. The customer feels much better, believes the job will be delivered on time, and stops worrying.

What did that printer do? He alleviated the customer's concern over a risk that didn't even exist.

A friend of mine owned a Japanese import car 30-some years ago. There weren't many dealers then, and not many of that particular make car in use here. He frequently had trouble getting parts when he needed them, sometimes waiting for weeks. So he switched to an American car.

Now he'd like to go back to the import model. There are many thousands of these cars on the road in this country now and hundreds of dealers—a dozen just in his own city. Parts are no longer a problem. Dealers get quick delivery from the maker. And if they need something even quicker, they can always get it from another dealer.

But my friend, remembering his experience in the 1950s, holds off going back to the import car because he's still afraid he'll have trouble getting parts when he needs them.

He made a decision to stay with his American car because of his concern over a risk that no longer exists.

How might a dealer handle my friend's worry over risk?

He could show him his organization's enormous parts inventory. He could show him part shipments from the maker—ordered a couple of days earlier. He could even flip through the Yellow Pages of the phone book, showing him the proliferation of agencies now selling that particular car, and explain how they get parts from each other when they are in a bind.

In summary:

Be more willing to take risks in negotiation; it pays off.

Be quick to remind the buyer, in a nice way, of the risks he may be taking in going with some company other than yours.

Deal effectively with risks the buyer perceives, even if those risks don't really exist.

7

The Power of Legitimacy

My friend has a small industrial rental unit. The first time he rented it he wrote out the lease. The tenant looked on, questioning every sentence, disputing every minor detail or reasonable statement.

Then a real estate man gave him advice: "You're crazy. Get the standard lease form. The tenant has virtually no rights."

"But won't the tenant object?"

"They sign it without looking at it—as long as you don't make a mark on it except your name."

And that's exactly what happened. Time after time.

Finally, one tenant had his lawyer brother-in-law look at the standard lease form before he signed it. "It abrogates most of my rights," he said.

"Everybody else just signs it without any changes," my friend said.

He said, "Aw, what the hell." And he signed it.

This is an example of the power of legitimacy. It is the most mystifying of the powers. It hypnotizes people.

There's this savings and loan institution in Los Angeles. If you walk in to get a loan they give you a piece of printed paper. It lists the principals of a number of loans: $10,000, $20,000, $30,000, and so on. For each one it specifies the down payment, the interest rate, and the number of years you have to pay it back.

Does this piece of paper make it hard for customers to negotiate? It certainly does.

The people at the bank say that before they had this printed, nearly everyone who came in for a loan felt it was negotiable—the down payment, or the interest rate, or the time period, or two or three of these.

Now they look at the sheet, nod their heads, make a choice, and accept it. The terms are all there, in black and white, a standard form. That must be the way it is. A simple piece of paper makes it hard for them to negotiate.

We tell this story in our Effective Negotiating seminar:

My father was in Mexico. He needed an auto part. He went to a parts store and saw what he needed. It had a price tag on it: $34.

He picked up the part, paid the $34, and left. Then he said to himself, "You jackass. You're probably the first person in months who paid the price tag price for a part in that store. And the last person who did it was probably an American, too."

For him, the price tag had the power of legitimacy. It ruled out negotiation in his mind.

Do you use a printed price list? A printed discount

sheet? Are your company policies and procedures about credit and delivery and such things in print—to show to your customers?

If your answers are yes, good for you; you're using the power of legitimacy. If your answers are negative, you're missing an important boat.

Suppose the customer asks you, "What is the price if I buy 1500 instead of 1000 units?" Is it helpful to have a printed sheet that shows the quantity discount price? Does it make it harder for the buyer to negotiate? Of course it does.

Suppose your company gives 30 days credit and a customer asks you for 60 days credit. You pull out your policies and procedures and show him the section that limits credit to 30 days. You can even give him a copy of it.

Then he can tell his boss he can't get the 60 days. If the boss asks why, he can point at the page. "It says so, right here."

Isn't it better for a printed page or standard form to say *no* to the customer than for you to say *no?* In addition, the piece of paper disarms him in terms of further negotiation.

Say you go to a lawyer to have a will made up. You ask the price. He pulls out his sheet from his state bar association. It says, "Wills. $400." Are you going to try to negotiate? Probably not.

That's the power of legitimacy. Its effect can be almost magical.

We go through life filling out forms without question, obeying signs without question, harking to rules and procedures without question. It's all part of the power of legitimacy.

Do buyers ever use the power of legitimacy when dealing with sellers? They sure do.

Has a government buyer ever said to you, "I'm sorry, the armed services procurement regulations don't permit that."

One seller, whenever he hears that, says, "But it doesn't apply in this case." He responds that way automatically. "It doesn't apply in this case." He puts doubt in the buyer's mind. He figures the buyer hasn't read the regulations in years, if he ever did read them.

Remember the show "Candid Camera" produced by Allen Funt? He once did a beautiful job of demonstrating the power of legitimacy.

Picture New York City at five o'clock in the afternoon—the rush hour. He had put a traffic light in the middle of the sidewalk at 42nd Street and Broadway. New Yorkers rushing along. The light in the middle of the sidewalk turns red. What do they do? They stop. They stop and stand there until it turns green. Then they go. The light turns red again and the next bunch of people stop and wait. Except for one man. He stops, looks to the right, then to the left, then runs on.

That traffic light—in the middle of the sidewalk, where it certainly didn't belong—had the power of legitimacy.

The printed price list, standard terms and conditions, the discount sheet, the standard forms, published procedures and policies—all these have the power of legitimacy, for you to use.

8

The Power of Knowledge

A plastics salesman who attended one of our seminars told this story:

He was in a new negotiation with a longtime customer. The buyer, nudging at the price, had a number of complaints. Breakage was higher than anticipated. One shipment had been two days late. The percentage of plastic molds with flaws was higher than they thought it would be.

A week earlier one of this salesman's support people had been talking to an end user at this company. The end user had said, "Boy, are we glad you guys are providing these. One of them breaks now and then. There've been some with flaws. But it's nothing compared to the last outfit they bought these from. They broke all the time. Their delivery trucks were always late. The service was lousy—they didn't even return our calls. They were a crappy outfit."

Was that information from the end user helpful to the

salesman in dealing with the buyer in that negotiation? Was it a source of power for him? Of course.

The buyer was doing his job. His complaints were legitimate ones. Voicing the complaints was a good way to try to get the price down.

But the salesman knew that the problems with his product were nothing compared to the problems they had with the previous supplier. And he negotiated with that in mind.

Knowledge is extremely important in negotiation. The more you know about your own product and your own company, the more you know about your competition, and, especially, the more you know about the buyer and his organization, the stronger your position.

Remember our salesman, Charlie Miller? He rushed into the negotiation feeling powerless and knocked down his price because there were so many things he didn't know.

They liked his product, his terms, his service, his proposal, and they liked him. He didn't know any of these things—and took no time to try to discover any of them. So he left $7020 on the table.

Before any negotiation, wouldn't it be helpful if you knew how the buyer's engineers feel about your product? . . . How much of a risk-taker the buyer is? . . . Whether he had bad experiences with any of your competitors? . . . If he has a pile of requisitions to fill and not much time to fill them? . . . Whether he is measured by numbers of orders placed or numbers of good negotiations? . . . Whether his non-negotiable policies are really non-negotiable? . . . How important the purchase is— whether the order you're about to negotiate is one percent of the material needed for the project, or 75 percent?

Would it be to your advantage if you knew the workings of the buyer's material control system? Wouldn't that mean you would know his needs before they come up, know if orders can be consolidated?

Suppose you know how much money the buyer has available for a purchase. Doesn't that give you an edge in negotiating?

Even more important, suppose you know the buyer's organization is going to be reimbursed by its customer for the goods. Whatever the cost, they're passing it on to their customer. Will that buyer be as determined to get the lowest price? Won't his resolve be less, his firmness less firm? Certainly.

Much of this kind of information comes not from the buyer, but from other people around in the buyer's organization. And often, other people in your organization can collect the information.

Some companies have a rule: Sellers cannot talk to their engineers. But can your engineers talk to their engineers? Probably. If they know what to ask, what kind of information to pick up, they can be powerful tools in negotiation.

We sellers are often in such a rush to get an order, we don't take the time to get the information that would make it a better order, a more profitable order.

One way to pick up information that will increase your power in negotiation is by listening—listening in the right way, that is. The good listener does it actively, not passively. He looks the speaker in the eye, encourages him to talk more and more, and learns more and more.

Most of us like to hear ourselves talk. Buyers are no exception. Encourage them to ramble on and on—important information can fall out in the most unlikely conversations. Don't interrupt. Don't argue. Don't be easily distracted. Listen. And learn.

One of the things sellers should be listening for is dumb remarks. You've made them. I've made them. Buyers make them.

Suppose the buyer lets you know he's desperate for your product, needs it in ten days. Isn't that dumb? Isn't he telling you he's not going to be much concerned with price?

Suppose the buyer comes out and says something like this: "We've looked around and your product is the best one for our needs." Doesn't that dumb remark increase your power in negotiation? Of course, but buyers sometimes do say things like that.

The more you know about the buyer and his organization the better you'll negotiate. At the same time, the less the buyer knows about the internal workings of your organization, the better your position.

Here's a true story involving a large aerospace company, the federal government, and a $500 million contract.

The government purchasing people were, of course, working to get the price down. The sales people negotiating for the aerospace firm hammered the point that the bid price was justified because part of the project would be extremely difficult to carry out.

An engineer, who was part of the aerospace team for technical reasons, suddenly commented: "Well, it won't be that difficult."

Needless to say, the price went down.

Did the aerospace negotiators want the buyers to know that it might not be *that* difficult? Hardly.

The power of knowing has two aspects:

1. Taking the time and making the effort to collect as much information as you can about the buyer and his organization.
2. Staying in tight control of the flow of information to the buyer about your organization.

When the aerospace engineer made his comment about the difficulty of a phase of that project, the aerospace negotiators lost control of the flow of information to the buyer . . . and lost money.

You should want to know a great many things. You should want the buyer to know only certain things.

Do you want the buyer to know your company's business is on the downslide and you desperately need his order? Of course not. Do you want him to know about your production problems? No. Do you want him to know cost breakdowns in regard to your product? Not if you can help it.

There are times when it's important to know when not to know. A buyer can't interrogate you about your company's cost breakdowns if you simply don't know anything about them. It's sometimes smart to be dumb.

9

The Power of Time

Time is money. We've all heard that expression for years. In negotiation, time is money in a different way. The more time you take, the more money you end up with, the more profit you end up with.

Time is the ultimate power. It's the key to the other powers.

Negotiation is a process of discovery for the sales person—discovering his powers. This takes time and the more time the seller takes, the more he discovers.

Negotiation begins days, weeks, and sometimes even months before you sit down at the bargaining table. And it may end months later. The better you use that time, the better negotiator you will be.

Time is the key that unlocks the seller's other powers. The power of knowing? It's, of course, a matter of taking the time to find out. The power of the competition and things that limit the buyer's ability to use the competition? You discover them by investing the time. The power of risk-taking demands time because risks must be recognized and calculated. The power of wooing? Again, an investment in time.

Turn time to your advantage—that's the key to better negotiation. Invest in time. Nothing pays better dividends.

You can't discover your powers if you don't take the time to look for them. And you must take the time to use them.

Charlie Miller made that mistake. He had a lot of things going for him but took no time and discovered none of them. Instead, he rushed in, cut his price, and left a lot of money behind him.

Remember Sam, the vice president, and Hank, the district manager? What was Sam saying to Hank? Something like this: "Hey, don't be so fast to argue for another discount. Stop and think—about our company, our products, our service, our good reputation. Remember your commitment to our organization and our business, our pride in them. Wait a minute, and think. We're worth the price we're asking, we know that. Use that commitment as a power."

We sellers are always in too much of a rush. Close the sale, close the sale, close the sale—we are told and tell ourselves. But what good is closing the sale if it's a lousy sale? Maybe we make a little commission, but the boss isn't happy, the company's making little or no profit. What good is that? We rush to make the sale and learn later there was no profit in it.

Remember what Sam said to Hank? "If we cut the price another 50 percent, we'd get plenty of orders. We'd be very busy—as we went out of business."

We sellers have to slow down. We have to stop and think. We have to use time.

A wise man once said, "Take time from the urgent to do the important." That expression fits us like a glove. We view making the sale as urgent. But taking the time to make it a *good* sale—that's important.

There's another way to use time as a power. That is, looking at it from the buyer's standpoint.

We're always concerned, and usually overly concerned, with our time pressures, our time problems, our quota problems—usually wrapped in time.

But doesn't the buyer have time problems and time pressures, too? Doesn't he have quotas, too? Usually. Sometimes the buyer's time pressures are greater than yours.

Suppose the engineers are hammering at the buyer: "Come on, man, let's get that stuff in here—we got to get going on this project." Doesn't that buyer have a time problem—one that works to your advantage?

Suppose the buyer's supervisor is leaning on the buyer: "Let's go, Harry. We've got a mountain of requisitions to fill before the end of the week. Let's get with it." Doesn't this buyer have a time problem that's a potential source of power to you?

Maybe it's the buyer's anniversary and he simply wants to clear his desk and get home a little early. Time works for you in that case.

The most powerful weapon in your arsenal as a seller is time. That's why we're going to discuss time—and time tactics—in more detail in a later chapter.

10

Shut Up: Safeguarding Your Power

In our Effective Negotiating® seminar we tell this story:

"The salesman gave me his proposal. I had just started to look at it, hadn't gotten past the first line, when he leaned over and said: 'We can do better than that.'"

Was that a dumb remark? It sure was.

Another salesman is in conversation with a buyer about his bid. He says to the buyer, "We have a surplus. We have to get rid of it."

Is that a dumb remark? Of course.

We've all made dumb remarks at one time or another. Dumb remarks weaken our power in negotiation. So the rule we have to remember is: *Know when to shut up.*

Know when to shut up, and you safeguard your power.

Have you ever told the buyer you had a large inventory? Or that your company was having a production problem, or billing foulups, or delivery snags? These all qualify as dumb remarks.

Here's another story from the Karrass seminar:

> BUYER: I need a 20-cent concession.
> SELLER: I can't do it.
> BUYER: Who can give it to me?
> SELLER: My boss can.
> BUYER: Will he give it to me?
> SELLER: Yes.

As sellers, we want to know as much as we possibly can about the buyer and his organization. But we want him to know as little as possible about the workings of our organizations. Dumb remarks reduce our powers in negotiation because they give information to the buyer—information we don't want him to have.

While we're shutting up, and avoiding dumb remarks about our companies and their operations, we should listen too—for dumb remarks by buyers.

Buyers make as many dumb remarks as sellers. Here are a few:

"We're desperate. We have to have it, and have it in two days or we're sunk."

"We agreed on five weeks' delivery but we have to have it in three weeks. We really must have it. How much extra will you charge for that?"

"Your product is the best by far. Our engineers say the others can't even compete with it."

Do those dumb remarks from buyers increase your power? Certainly. If the buyer is desperate, he's not likely to quibble about price. If he asks you how much you'll charge for earlier delivery, he's inviting that extra charge. If he tells you your product virtually has no competition, he's strengthening your negotiating position enormously.

Dumb remarks emanate from sources other than buyers and sellers. These dumb remarks, made by non-negotiators, can have a profound effect on seller–buyer negotiations.

If an engineer at the customer location tells one of your engineers that he loves your product, and this comment is relayed to you, that puts you in a very strong position at the next negotiation with that company's buyer. On the other hand, if your engineer tells an engineer of the customer firm about all the problems encountered getting your product finally working, that can cripple your negotiation power.

Engineers talk to engineers, accountants talk to accountants, manufacturing people talk to manufacturing people, management talks to management, and even very top management talks to very top management.

And they all make dumb remarks sometimes. As a matter of fact, it's probably true that more dumb remarks, which have a profound effect on negotiations, are made by non-negotiators than by negotiators. And these dumb remaks can stretch out in time.

A dumb remark made by someone in your organization to someone in the buyer organization in January can hurt you when you sit down at the bargaining table in June. In effect, the negotiation actually began the day of that dumb remark in January.

To avoid that kind of weakening of our negotiation powers, we must know when to shut up—and others in our organization must know when to shut up.

There's one time when it's especially important to shut up. That's when the buyer asks for a cost breakdown.

Buyers love cost breakdowns from sellers, and for good reason. A cost breakdown tells the buyer what profit is built into your proposal—how far he can go in nudging your price. It also tells him your material costs. This means he could shop the material elsewhere, and perhaps save money.

The rule is: Never give a cost breakdown unless required by law.

The subject of shutting up and avoiding dumb remarks has one other aspect. That is, how to elicit dumb remarks from buyers—remarks that will strengthen your negotiation position. We take up this subject later in the book.

II

Tactics for Handling Tactics

11

Seek and Ye Shall Find

If you look for garbage, you find it.

That's true in selling, it's true in sales negotiation, and it's true in just about every aspect of our lives.

We may not realize it. But most of what we hear is just plain garbage.

Our prices are too steep, our competition is keen, our products could be better. Isn't that the kind of thing we hear all day long? The problem is that after a while we begin to believe it, listen for it, and find it.

We hear what we're listening for, we find what we're looking for. Our jobs as sellers train us to listen for garbage, to find garbage. And the buyer is always there to help us find any we may have missed. That's his job. That's what he gets paid to do.

We can always find the garbage, if that's what we're looking for. It's easy.

If we look for problems with our children, can we find

them? Certainly. No child is completely without problems. If we look for things wrong with our spouses, can we find things wrong? Sure. Nobody's perfect.

Say you've heard that people in Paris are rude. You go to Paris looking for rude people—will you find them? Sure, there are eight million people in Paris. You're bound to find plenty of rude ones.

Suppose you have an American car. You hear a lot of negative things about American cars. You get down on American cars. Yours breaks down. What do you do? You curse American cars.

You buy an imported car. Something goes wrong. What do you do? You say well, things do go wrong. Or maybe you blame the American roads.

We hear what we want to hear, we see what we want to see, we believe what we want to believe.

If you're looking for an employee to foul up, sooner or later he will. He'll do something not quite the way you wanted it done. If you look for reasons why you should quit your job, you can find them. Every job has plusses and minuses. If you have a feeling you're not going to make the sale, you can listen for, pick up, and store information that validates that feeling.

There was an interesting experiment involving a school teacher and a group of children. The pupils were all about average, but she was told that some were bright and some were slow. What happened? Those she expected to be bright tended to do well; those she expected to be slow tended to do not so well.

We find what we're looking for.

If you want to find reasons to be depressed can you find them? Easily. There are reasons for depression in all our lives and we can concentrate on them if we choose to. The fact is, they usually make up just one aspect of our lives. And there are many aspects, and chances are they're in balance.

A friend of mine who's a psychotherapist once said, "There's always a garbage truck going to the dump—if you want to get on it. If you're looking for one to get on it'll be there. But the question is, what do you want to do?"

We said in an earlier chapter that most of our experience as sales people is not making the sale. Most of what we hear as sales people is negative—complaints about our products and our prices, compliments paid our competition.

Often even when a buyer is placing an order, he's still objecting to our price, or belittling our product, or saying he can do better with the competition.

Yes, there's always a garbage truck going to the dump, if we want to get on it.

The mistake we make as sellers is hearing and believing the garbage. More than that, we specifically listen for it, specifically look for it. We make the mistake of collecting it, gathering it as ammunition to call the product manager and argue for a lower price.

What we forget is that the buyer will object to the price whether he has a price objection or not. That's what he's supposed to do. He will try to get the price down even if he doesn't think it's too high. That's what he's supposed to do.

The people in the buyer's organization will never forgive him if he does not *try* to get a lower price. But they will always forgive him if he doesn't get it.

So the buyer always has to try for the lower price—

whether or not he needs it or wants it or even thinks it's justified.

Not long ago I was interested in buying a new word processing system and a friend had recommended a particular brand to me.

I knew I was going to buy this one, I didn't want the hassle of shopping around.

The salesman demonstrated the system. It seemed fine, and the price was okay. I had the money in the budget. It seemed like a fair buy, but price was not really important.

But just as a matter of routine, and because my general manager was present, I suggested the price—$3300—was a little steep for me. Doing that was my job.

"I'll see what I can do and call you in a week," the salesman said.

A week went by. The salesman called and said he could sell me the system for $2700. I thanked him and hesitated, then said I'd think about it.

Why, I wondered, did he lower his price so much?

Two days later he called again. I could have the system for $2400.

How did I react? Negatively. The system had been highly recommended to me. It looked fine in the demonstration, I had no real problem with the original price. I wanted to buy it.

But now I was concerned. Why did he lower the price so much, and so much a second time? Was there something wrong with the product, or with the company? I decided I'd have to look into other, competitive systems, and I did.

I questioned that salesman's original price because that was what I was supposed to do. He took that as a serious price objection, lowered his price too much and too often, and scared me off.

That salesman was looking for garbage and he found it. And that's the way it is. Listen for garbage, and there's plenty around to hear. Look for garbage and there's plenty around to see.

Our senses are tuned: we hear what we want to hear, we see what we want to see. And *we* do the tuning—just like the dial on our radios.

Let's say you and I go to an orchestra concert. I am more interested in brass than you; you are more interested in strings than I am. What will the result be?

I will hear the brass better than you do. You will hear the strings better than I do.

Take this one step further. Suppose a friend told you he heard the concert the night before and the strings screwed up along the way. You will not only be especially listening for the strings, but especially listening for them to screw up. And if they do, you will certainly hear them do it. I probably won't. I'll be enjoying the brass.

Negotiation is an experience in human relations. Human relations are like the full orchestra because there are so many component parts making up the whole thing.

Just as we can hear the sections of the orchestra best that we want to hear best—or worst, as the case may be— we find the components of negotiation that we look for. And if we look for garbage we find it, every time.

It will be there in negotiation—comments about our high prices, complaints about our product, compliments about our competition. Expect that, assume that.

And it's tougher in negotiation to tune out the garbage than it is in other areas of our lives, for two reasons. One is that we don't go in objectively—we go in expecting to hear more of the same kind of negative things we've been hearing all week. The other reason is the buyer: he's there to make sure we find the garbage, make sure we hear it. That's his job.

If you get overly concerned with negative aspects of your life and go to a psychotherapist, his job is to turn you around, to point out the good things in your life, to bring you back into balance.

The buyer does just the opposite. You go into negotiation already feeling your prices are too high, your product's not good enough, your competition is terrific. The buyer's there to tell you how right you are, and, as a matter of fact, your prices are even higher than you thought they were, your product worse than you thought it was, your competition even better than you thought it was.

This is why realizing your source of power is so important.

Your only defense in this tough situation is tuning in to your potential sources of power, staying at that frequency, listening for clues to information that bolsters those sources of power.

Don't go into a negotiation listening for the garbage, ready to believe it—again. Listen for hints to things that limit the buyer's ability to use the competition. Look for clues to the time pressures or problems the buyer may be confronting. Listen for clues to what other people in the buyer's organization may think of your product. Listen for all the things you may have going *for* you, things that strengthen your negotiation position.

It takes some effort. It takes a strong realization of your potential sources of power, and how they can work for

you. This realization must be foremost in your mind because the buyer will be doing his best to help you find the
garbage. Again, that's his job. That's what he's there for.
He will be using a variety of tactics, approaches, maneuvers, to accomplish this.

We discuss these tactics next.

12

How the Buyer Helps You Find It

The buyer has a bagful of tactics he uses to help us sellers find the garbage. The better the buyer, the more adept he is at using them.

Too often, we fall for them. That's why the buyer uses these tactics. They usually work.

First, we're going to talk about three of the most common, most successful buyer tactics. Then we'll discuss the countermeasures, how we can deal with these tactics. Then we'll explore some additional buyer maneuvers that are also tactics.

Two of these first three tactics are seductive. They, in effect, woo us. The other is nonseductive, often abusive. It annoys or even angers us.

But they all work, too frequently.

Is the buyer who uses these tactics a bad person? No. He's doing the job he's paid to do. The point is, to what extent do we want to help him?

His job is getting the best possible product at the lowest

possible price. His job is getting us sellers to lower our prices—and make other concessions as well.

Our job is not just to close the sale but to close sales that mean some profit for the organizations that employ us. Otherwise, why bother?

To do our job, we must recognize buyer moves that are tactics and identify them as tactics. Then we can sort out the countermeasures at our command, pick those that work with that particular tactic—and deal with the tactic.

The first tactic we're going to expose and explore, one of the more seductive and more successful ones, is the *bogey*. It has a couple of variations.

You're familiar with it. You've heard it many times. It's this one: "I love your product. It's beautiful. It's just what I need. It works like a charm. But the price is $100,000 and I only have $80,000. That's all there is. There is no more. That's all I have."

It's polite. It's complimentary. And it's final. Or so it seems.

How do we react? We fall for it. He hasn't knocked our product, or our price. He's played to our ego. He's come to us with a problem—he has just so much money. He's come to us for help. We immediately think, well now let's see if there's some way we can work this out.

Suppose you've proposed a room addition for my house —at $40,000. I try the bogey. I say, "It's ideal. It's just what we need, in every way. But I only have $30,000. The bank would only give me $30,000. That's all there is. I don't have another dollar to add to it."

Do you resent me? No. You resent the bank. You wish they'd given me $10,000 more. But you want to help me. You want to work with me.

To begin with, will I, the buyer, learn if there's some

slack in your bid? Probably. And I'll learn a great deal more.

Maybe you suggest a certain saving if you use a different type of faucet in the bathroom, and a cheaper kind of tile. Maybe you tell me you have $500 in the bid for painting and, if I want to do it myself, I can save that.

I use the bogey and all kinds of information starts falling in my lap, information that you, the seller, probably didn't want to give me.

After a time, I have gathered what nearly amounts to your cost breakdown for your bid. What does that tell me? It tells me how far I can push, how far down you can go—and still make a profit.

You have virtually taught me how to do the job cheaper. And that means this: you will make less money. Maybe you've also taught me how to deal more effectively and more knowledgeably if I get bids from other vendors—your competition. And that means you might not get the job at all.

Let's say I want to build a swimming pool and I get bids from you and a number of other vendors.

I call you in and I say, "Your plan is the perfect pool for our family, for our house. I wouldn't change a thing. It's ideal.

"But your price is $27,000 and all I have is $25,000—and that has to include not just the pool but the necessary fencing and the landscaping and the redwood deck at the end."

I show you a certified check for $25,000, saying, "My uncle left me this money in his will. That's the whole thing. I can't take on any debts to do this project. I have to do it all with this amount."

Have I said anything to put you off or annoy you? No.

I've complimented you. I've told you your proposed pool is the best solution, the best plan. I've made you feel good about that. I've also made it plain that I only have $25,000 and that it has to cover things besides your pool. I've made it plain I can't go over that figure.

Isn't it likely that you will take a second, closer look at your bid, to see if it can be shaved? Might you not also start telling what items I could eliminate or change to save this amount or that amount? Is it possible you will tell me how I might subcontract some of the additional things myself, and save money that way?

I've used the bogey tactic on you and because I have, you're helping me get your price down. You're helping me do things more economically.

You are, in effect, helping me negotiate.

How about *the budget?* Isn't that a bogey?

You bid $1 a pound and I say, "Sounds fine to me but I have this budget and there's only 92 cents a pound in the budget." I show you the budget and I point to the line and, sure enough, it says 92 cents a pound.

Do you have any reason to be annoyed with me? No. I don't have any problem with your product, or your price. But I have this budget and it says 92 cents a pound. There it is, on paper. What can I do about it? I look helpless and within seconds you're trying to figure out how to help me do business with you within my budget.

You're angry, but not at me. You're annoyed with a piece of paper that has 92 cents a pound printed on it. You have to deal with that piece of paper. You have to help me deal with it. Soon you're helping me figure out how I can get what I want for 92 cents a pound.

I used the bogey, and you went for it.

There's another kind of bogey—your own. You don't

mean to create your own bogey, of course. But you do. You get trapped into it. And, later, it turns around and bites you. It works this way.

I'm the buyer and I call you up and say, "Listen, management is making this demand of me. I need a price, a quote—a planning purpose quote. You don't have to be right, or exact, just a ballpark figure. But I need one.

"It would be for 1000 units. Like that thing you made for us last year, but a little different. We don't have the specs yet, but I have to have some kind of quote for planning purposes."

Suppose you give me your planning purpose quote: $100 a unit. You tell me it's a ballpark number. You tell me I shouldn't hold you to it.

Three months later I send you a formal request for proposal. You see the specs now. It's like the thing you did the year before, but a little more complicated. Your bid is $110 a unit.

I call you up. What do I say? I say you told me it was going to be $100. I tell you I gave that number to my accounting people. Now you come up with $110. You've given me a problem. What happened to the $100?

You've been trapped by your own bogey. No matter what you say, I've got that $100 in my head and it will be very hard for you to dislodge it. You told me $100. Now, if I can't get $100 I'll look like a jerk to my people. Why do you want to do that to me?

Now, to another seductive buyer tactic: the *Krunch*.

Remember in Chapter 1 we spent a week making calls with salesman Charlie Miller? Remember the prospect at the pest control company who was interested in several desktop copying machines and a printing system?

Charlie made his pitch, outlined his proposed solution for the customer's needs, and threw in a ten percent discount.

The buyer looked at Charlie and said, "You've got to do better than that." Then he turned away.

This is the tactic we call the Krunch. It's short and simple. It's effective. It works on us.

"You've got to do better than that." What's so magical about these words? Why do they so often help the buyer get a lower price?

One buyer I know uses the Krunch another way. He just says, "You're close." Just those two words. "You're close." No seller assumes he's close low. He assumes he's close, but high.

How does the seller react? Well, its not all negative. He's in the running. The buyer's willing to consider doing business with him. That's better than the last three. They just said no.

He also says to himself, yes, he's right, our prices are too high.

We sales people don't have much faith in our organization's pricing structure. At our negotiation seminars we ask those attending to rate their confidence in their company's pricing system on a scale from 0 to 10—zero being no confidence, ten being great confidence.

Most rate it at a two or three; no one ever rates it as high as six.

So when the buyer says, "You've got to do better than that," the seller says to himself, "I knew all along we had to do better than that."

Then the seller goes to his manager and repeats it: "We've got to do better than that."

The manager asks, "Why?"

The seller replies, "Because he told me we've got to do better than that."

"Oh, he did," the manager replies. After all, that makes sense. He was out in the field selling for years, he heard those words a thousand times, so he agrees. Together they go to their pricing people and tell them, "We've got to do better than that."

And they do. Using the Krunch, the buyer has played on the seller's lack of confidence in his prices, and helped him go back to his own organization—for a lower price.

The Krunch is successful for that very reason. When the buyer says, "You've got to do better than that," the seller agrees with the buyer. And he does better than that.

Remember what happened to Charlie? When the buyer at the pest control company used those magic words on him, Charlie argued with the people in his home office and got another discount. Then he called the buyer with the good news. What did the buyer say?

He said they'd decided to farm out their copying and printing, even though it would be more expensive. They didn't want the machines cluttering up the office.

That buyer's problem was not with price at all. It was with space. Nevertheless, it was his job to try and get a lower price anyway, and he used the Krunch to do it.

Charlie spent his time arguing with his people for a lower price. If he had spent his time differently, prolonging discussion with the customer, listening, probing, the space issue would probably have emerged. And he could have shown the customer how to accommodate his machines and still economize on space.

In our Effective Negotiating seminars we bring up another variation of the Krunch: "You've got to do *significantly* better than that."

Someday we would like to do an experiment—telling one control group, "You've got to do better than that," and telling the other group, "You've got to do significantly better than that."

Our guess, and it's probably a good one, is that we'd get even lower prices from the second group—because of that one word, *significantly*.

The next tactic is a nonseductive one that buyers use. It's also an abrupt one, and commonly abusive. It's these five words: *Take it or leave it.*

It leaves us feeling helpless. It leaves us feeling we have only two choices, like the buyer said: to take it or leave it.

It goes like this:

"Your company's not dependable. Your product's not that good. I don't have time to screw around. This is what I'll pay—take it or leave it. If you don't want the order, fine. No problem. I'll get it somewhere else."

Or:

"You come here with a price increase. There's no way I'm going to pay it. If you want to give it to me at the old price, fine. If not, forget it. I don't have time to sit here talking about it. That's what I'll pay. You can have the order or not have it. Makes no difference to me."

Or:

"My cost analysis people tell me they know you can make the thing at that price and make a profit. So that's our bottom line number. If you don't want it, I'll find someone who does. But remember, times are bad. I'd advise you to take it."

Or:

"Here's what we need. Here's what we'll pay. Don't tell me about your terrific company, don't tell me about your great service. I've no time for all that crap. Do it at our price, and you got the order. You don't want to do it at that price, you don't have the order. I've got vendors lined up out there. Make up your mind."

13

Countermeasures at Your Command

Why do we give tactics names? We've talked about the bogey, the Krunch, the take it or leave it. We'll be talking about more tactics later. They'll have names, too.

We give the tactics names because that makes it easier for us to spot them, tag them as tactics, and deal with them. This is important because they never appear in negotiation as tactics. They appear as non-negotiable issues. But they rarely are.

This is one lesson I learned when I was still a kid.

I was in my senior year in high school. My biggest goal in life? To own a Ford Mustang. I desperately wanted a Ford Mustang. I saved my money, read the car ads, saved more money.

Then I saw this ad: *1966 black Ford Mustang convertible. $800.*

It was just what I wanted. I could handle the $800. I called and made an appointment to see the car.

I drove to the address in Bel Air. It was a big house, nearly a mansion. There was a circular drive in front and the Mustang was parked there. It was beautiful. I saw myself starting college in the fall—a guy with a Mustang convertible.

I drove the car. I loved it. I asked the owner if I could have a mechanic check it over. He said sure, leave $400 deposit and take it to a Ford mechanic. He gave me his card. He was an attorney with offices in Century City, a fashionable Los Angeles business center.

The car checked out. I called the attorney and said I wanted to buy it. He said fine, come by the office.

That afternoon I was in his plush office, ready to take the $400 balance out of my pocket when he suddenly said, "I've decided I have to have $850 for the car. The price is $850."

My heart sank. I was crushed. The $800 was every dollar I had. I saw my social life going down the tubes.

"I don't have that much with me," I said, finally. "Hold the deposit. Don't sell the car. Let me see if I can get it." And I left.

I couldn't wait for my father to come home that night. As soon as he walked in the house I told him. "He has to have $850 for the Mustang. Can you loan me $50?"

My father thought for a moment, then said, "Maybe he has to have $850. Maybe he doesn't. It's a tactic. There are ways to deal with it. There are countermeasures. Go back and say you just can't raise the other $50. And there are other countermeasures . . ."

I interrupted him. "I want the car. If I don't come up with the $850, he won't sell it to me. I don't need tactics and countermeasures. I need $50. Will you loan it to me?"

He did. I went back, gave the attorney the $450 balance, and drove off in the car.

Was I wrong? About as wrong as a person can get. That attorney used a tactic called *Escalation* on me. We'll be discussing it a little later. But instead of recognizing it as a tactic—or even listening to my father, who did recognize it as a tactic—I panicked. I saw my whole future as a big man on campus in a Mustang going up in smoke because of $50. And I paid the escalated price without question.

Suppose I had gone back to him and said, "I'm sorry. I just can't raise another $50. This $800 is all I have, all I can get together." I would have been using the bogey tactic as a countermeasure.

Would it have been worth his while to refuse the $800 and readvertise the car, and spend more time showing it— on the chance he might get another $50 for it? Hardly. Chances are, he would have taken the $800.

Or, I could have done something else. I was a high school kid. I looked kind of grubby, anyway. I could have put on my most ragged jeans, tennis shoes and no socks, a holey T-shirt with words of questionable taste printed on them.

I could have gone back to his swanky office and sat around the waiting room, starting dopey conversations with his waiting clients.

When I got in his office, I could have been as inarticulate as a person can get. Like, "I don't understand. You said the price was $800. It was in the paper. Now you say $850. I don't understand what the $50 is. I mean, here's the paper. See, it says $800. I don't understand." I could have dragged out that conversation almost incoherently.

How long do you think it would have been before he

said, "Okay, give me the $400 balance. Take the car and get out of here." Probably, not very long.

The point is, we have to recognize tactics as tactics before we can deal with them. They appear to us as non-negotiation issues. We have to isolate and tag the tactic, then figure out how to counter it.

When the attorney told me the price was $850, I saw no alternatives. I thought: *Either I come up with the additional $50 or I lose the car.*

That happens to us in sales. The buyer says he needs another four percent discount and we see no alternatives. We think: *We get the four percent for him or we lose the sale.*

When I told my father about the $850 price for the Mustang he immediately identified the move as a tactic and, just as quickly, possible countermeasures began coming to his mind. He saw a number of alternatives.

Negotiation is a game. A serious one, but still a game. Once we realize that, we can learn how to play it expertly. And by viewing it that way we remove the emotion, remove the anger, remove the hostility from our minds. These negative feelings do not help us to be better negotiators. They hamper our negotiation skills.

Now, when I'm talking to a buyer and he uses a tactic, how do I respond? Let's say he uses the bogey. He says, "But I only have $5000 in the budget for this. That's the absolute limit."

I train myself to say to myself, "Hey, good choice. He used the bogey. Terrific. He's doing his job. The bogey was a good selection. Great selection. I wouldn't mind having him in my organization as a buyer. I certainly wouldn't want a buyer who immediately said to the seller, 'Okay, the price is fine. I'll buy it.' "

I train myself to spot the tactic as a tactic, and tag it, and isolate it. Then I can stand aside and look at the tactic as his approach to negotiation. If I don't train myself to do that, how do I react? I say to myself, oh crap, here's another buyer who's not going to buy. I get discouraged, negative, I feel I have no alternatives but to lower my price, or walk away.

But by isolating the tactic, I take the emotion out of the situation. It frees my mind then to think about counter-measures, ways to deal efficiently with the tactic. It's round one, the first inning. The game is on.

For example—let's look at the buyer tactic "take it or leave it."

Negotiation training is important because we live in a world of take it or leave its. Department store prices, su-permarket prices—they cry out *take it or leave it* to us all the time. Every month we get our telephone bills, our water, gas, electric bills. What do they say to us? Take it or leave it. Pay this price or you don't have a phone. Period.

Because we're surrounded by this kind of take it or leave it in our culture, we think that all take it or leave its are non-negotiable. We begin to look upon them as part of our physical world—about as negotiable as the law of gravity.

This is wrong. When the Vietnamese refugees came to this country in the mid-1970s they looked upon super-market prices as negotiable. And they tried to negotiate. It was their culture. And, in Texas, they eventually did succeed in negotiating prices in supermarket produce de-partments.

Business take it or leave its are not like the laws of physics. They're man-made—and subject to change.

If your price is $110 a unit and the buyer says he can only pay $100 a unit, that $100 figure wasn't sent down to him by a higher being. Chances are it was the result of an earlier internal negotiation, between him, his engineer, and his cost analyst. Maybe the engineer said your product was good, and worked, and was worth $110. Maybe the cost analyst said the way he figured it, you could sell it for $95 and still make a profit. Maybe the buyer picked $100 as the target, and the three settled on that.

So the $100 figure the buyer quotes you was the result of negotiation. And anything that is the result of negotiation can be renegotiated.

Remember we said in the first chapter that negotiation is a process during which all kinds of things happen and all kinds of things change? One of the things that changes is what the other party wants or needs. We call this the *forever-for-now* concept.

When the buyer says he will only spend a certain amount, it's true, at the moment he says it. It is true forever-for-now. A few minutes later, his mind may change. That amount may change. A new amount becomes what he wants forever. But forever-for-now.

Not long ago I went to buy an answering machine. I knew the make and model I wanted. I had made up my mind. I didn't go to look and wonder. I went to buy a particular model at a particular price—$150. I knew what I wanted.

Then the salesman showed me some other models, with other features. They were features I hadn't considered, features I could use. I changed my mind. My want changed.

When I went to the store I wanted a certain machine at

a certain price. It was true forever in my mind. But it was what I wanted forever—for now. Within a few minutes, after looking at the more expensive model, there was a new want. I wanted *that* one. And I bought it. For $250.

In negotiation, truth shifts, moves around. What is true at one moment may disappear and within minutes there is a different truth. It doesn't mean the first truth wasn't valid. It means it was true forever—for now.

I had an office space to lease. I calculated and arrived at a price: $2100. I wanted $2100 for the space. I did not want less. I would not take less.

Two weeks later my office space was still vacant. There were no takers at $2100. I arrived at a new want: $1900. I wanted $1900. I wouldn't take less.

At this writing the space is still vacant. And my new want of $1900 is getting a little shaky.

We have a friend and whenever he buys a suit he does this. He says if he buys the suit he wants a free tie, or he won't buy the suit. That stand is a truth to him when he says it. And he gets a lot of free ties that way.

But sometimes the men's store clerk declines. He says no, it's not their policy to give away ties. What does my friend do? He buys the suit anyway. His position—that he would buy the suit only if he got the free tie—was true in his mind forever, when he said it. Forever-for-now.

When he learned he was not going to get the free tie, his truth changed.

We sellers run into a lot of that in negotiation. It's a tactic called *nibbling*. The buyer says if he buys this, will you throw in that? Or if he pays this price, will you forget the tax? Or absorb the shipping charge.

Nibbling is that little push for something extra, something more. If you cannot give that something more, does that necessarily mean the buyer won't do business with you? No. If my friend likes the suit he buys it. He won't deny himself the suit just because he can't get a free tie.

I run into the bogey selling our two-day seminars. A training director calls, tells me how many people he wants to attend, and I calculate a price. Let's say it's $3500.

He says, "I only have $3000 in the training budget for this. That's all I can spend. That's it." And that's true in his mind. True forever-for-now.

Again, when I hear this I train myself to say to myself, "Hey, that's the bogey. Good choice. Now how do I deal with it?"

I try to keep talking. I tell him more and more about the seminar, what his people will save the first week after attending it. I tell him about all the Fortune 500 companies that license it.

He begins to think more and more of the idea of his people attending the seminar. He wishes he had more than $3000. He wishes he could make the $3500.

I try to talk and talk, string out the conversation. Eventually it comes out that he does, indeed, only have $3000 in his training budget for the seminar. But he also has a travel budget and a publications budget. And since our seminar involves travel and books as well as other materials, he can quite appropriately dip into these budgets.

If I had accepted his $3000 bogey as written in concrete, I would have had two choices: take the $3000 or lose the business.

If I had accepted his bogey as unchangeable, as being true forever, I would never have discovered alternatives. He would never have discovered alternatives.

But, because I made myself persist, alternatives emerged.

Are there other ways to counteract the bogey? Other countermeasures that can be used? Yes.

I could have changed the finances involved. I could have stuck to the $3500 price but said, "You can pay half in 30 days and the other half in 60 days." Might that have made a difference? It might have.

One seller I know always has a plan A and a plan B. If he had been in that bogey situation, for example, he might have handled it this way.

When the buyer said he had only $3000 for the two-day seminar, and couldn't handle the $3500 price, he would have proposed a one-day seminar instead, at a lower price.

This is changing the product, and the concept can be applied to most products. Maybe there's a feature the particular buyer doesn't really need, and the seller can eliminate that feature, and accommodate the bogey without losing money.

Sometimes sellers can change the design, the packaging, or the delivery, to deal with the bogey.

A sales woman who attended our seminar told us she sometimes handled that situation by reducing the cost of the packaging and delivery. She says, "We can do it at your price—if we package it economically, and you pick it up with your trucks." And that, she says, often works.

Sometimes budgets can be made bigger. Many a buyer has decided he really wanted or really needed a product that simply cost more than the allotted amount—and negotiated with his people for a higher budget.

Budgets, and other bogeys, are born in the minds of people, and people change their minds. Or, as we said before, anything that is the result of negotiation can be renegotiated.

III

Satisfying Without Giving In

14

Befriending Time

When I was a teenager my father did a great deal of traveling around the country presenting his seminar on Effective Negotiating. He was frequently gone for weeks at a time.

Whenever he returned from a trip I would barely give him time to get in the house and unpack before I would bombard him with my latest brainstorms. I'd decided I wanted to tour Europe, or I'd decided I wanted to go to law school, or to Mexico. Or I wanted to do this and go there or be that and go somewhere else, or do the other. Usually I hit him with a number of ideas at once.

How did he react? As though I was a crazy kid.

Then one time when he came home and I blurted out my latest schemes he looked at me for a moment, then said:

"My ideas are my old friends and your ideas are your friends. You may have some very good friends. But you cannot expect me to throw away my friends and adopt your friends at a moment's notice, as soon as you introduce them to me. Give me time to get used to them and I may adopt them. But I need that time—I need that acceptance time."

The matter of acceptance time, and the general concept of time, are extremely important in negotiation. Your friend may be a price of $1 a pound and the buyer's friend may be a price of 90 cents a pound. But if you give the buyer enough acceptance time, and handle that time properly, he may well discard his friend in favor of your friend.

Time is money. We've said it before and we say it again here because that three-word sentence is probably the most important statement in this book. The more time you invest in the negotiation, the better you come out. It's axiomatic. It's a rule. You can put that in the bank—literally.

Early in the book we stepped through the sales person's sources of power in negotiation. Only with time can you discover what powers are most useful in any particular negotiation, and how best to put those powers to work for you in that negotiation.

We've talked about buyer tactics, tactics generally aimed at knocking the quality of your product, boosting your competition, getting your prices down. We talked about countermeasures at your command in dealing with these tactics. And all these countermeasures involve time: time to choose, time to use.

Remember my experience buying an answering machine? I had my mind made up. I knew I wanted the simple $150 model. I went to the store to buy it. Period. No indecision, no questions, no doubts. I knew what I wanted and went to get it.

It would have been very easy for that salesman to have just wrapped up the $150 machine and sent me on my way, and he would have been happy to have made the sale. But he did better. He did more. He took time. He showed me the more expensive models, explained their features, outlined their advantages.

You know what happened. I walked out with the $250 model. That sales person took the time to steer me toward changing my want, then gave me the time to do it. It was, you will recall, the forever-for-now concept at work.

When I went to the store I wanted the $150 machine. That was true forever—but forever-for-now. Half an hour later I wanted the $250 machine. A new want had deposed the old want.

We sales people are in too much of a hurry too much of the time. Close the sale, close the sale, close the sale. We get that from above and we tell ourselves that. And when we're in too much of a hurry we don't give buyer wants time to change. We don't give the forever-for-now concept time to work. And we may close the sale. But we leave money on the table, money that is, as we've said before, pure profit.

A salesman friend of mine has a bold sign on the wall in front of his desk with these two words: BEFRIEND TIME. It's a constant reminder to him that, in negotiation, time is his strongest weapon, his most faithful ally.

Time enables you to realize your sources of power in negotiation, helps you spot and identify buyer tactics, helps you consider and use countermeasures to those tactics, and enables buyer wants to change during negotiation.

Time does something else: it helps you discover what the buyer really wants—besides the product and price he's talking about. And, in this way, time helps you navigate a very important iceberg in negotiation.

The tip of the iceberg? Price. The bulk of the iceberg? A constellation of human wants and needs—all of which affect price.

Price is always on the table in negotiation. Buyers like to talk price. And it almost always appears the most important issue and, often, the only issue. But it rarely is either.

If we look at the iceberg as what the buyer really wants and needs, the tip—always highly visible—represents price. But the tip, however prominent, is a small part of the whole iceberg, most of which lies beneath the surface. It is the sales person's job to take the time to discover the overall dimensions of this iceberg of buyer wants—and navigate them to closing.

These wants, which never appear on purchase orders, are as important as those items that do because they are "satisfiers." They contribute to the buyer's satisfaction. They affect price; many are more important than price.

Here are these satisfiers:

The buyer wants to feel he is competent and has good taste. Suppose the buyer makes a purchase but later feels the price he paid was a little high. Then users of the product compliment him on its quality, its appearance, its function. Does his worry about the price disappear? Usually. His feelings of competence and good taste have been reinforced—the importance of price diminished.

The buyer wants to avoid risk and trouble. If he can buy from your established, reliable firm without worry—over quality or delivery or support, for example—will he take a chance on a fly-by-night outfit just because its prices are lower? Hardly.

The buyer wants to look good in his own organization. He wants job security. If dealing with you will help him achieve these goals, will that affect price? Certainly.

The buyer wants relief from unnecessary work. If doing business with you is easier for him than doing business with your competition, won't that affect his decisions? Of course. The sales person who has the reputation of being easy to do business with has an edge. The buyer will pay more to do business with a vendor if he knows he'll have less hassle, less work.

The buyer wants to get it over with. He wants to move on to other transactions, other purchase problems. Does this affect buyer decisions? Of course. You've heard buyers say they were accepting your price because they just didn't have time to do more shopping around. Or, if doing business with you is simply faster and more efficient than doing business with others, that affects their decision.

The buyer wants to be considered fair and nice. Any time you can enhance the buyer's ego, build his self-esteem, take advantage of the opportunity. It will be a plus in your favor.

The buyer wants to add to his knowledge. Buyers rarely get away from their desks; sales people are in circulation. Whenever you can share with him business knowledge you pick up in your rounds, do so. It may involve product news or development, trends in technology or pricing or the marketplace. Whatever the subject, if you contribute to the buyer's knowledge—helping him do his job better—he will appreciate it.

The buyer often needs help in making hard purchasing decisions.

Dr. Karrass in his Effective Negotiating seminar tells about the time when he needed a new heating system for his house. He got four bids from four different companies. The prices ranged from $2100 to $6000.

"I sat down with the four quotes to compare apples and found there were no apples," he recalls. They were all proposing different systems, comprising different components, designed to do somewhat different things. I didn't know much about heating systems and had no real basis for comparison.

"I called the four companies and asked them to come out and explain their quotes. They all had excuses. They had all invested probably 14 to 16 hours in their proposals. They had come out, crawled around the attic, measured the place this way and that way. But they didn't want to take time to explain their proposals.

"Finally, the guy from one of the companies said he'd come. He did, and he explained his company's proposal and quote. But what about the other quotes? Rule number one is you don't show one vendor the bids of other vendors. Well, rule number one went out the window. I showed them all to him, and he explained them all.

"He got the order. I don't know to this day if it was the best decision. But he took the trouble to come out and help me make what for me was a hard decision, so he got the order."

We sellers often assume the buyer knows exactly what he wants and needs no help in making his decision. The opposite is often true. Many buyers deal with many products, many technologies. They cannot possibly keep up with them all.

The sales person who sincerely offers information or interpretation or opinion that helps the buyer make a decision has an edge. The sales person who helps the buyer in this way also learns more about the buyer, and hi, organization.

The buyer needs help if he gets in trouble. The seller who runs the other way when problems crop up doesn't keep the business very long. On the other hand, the sales person who is there to help the buyer when the product fails, or the system goes down, or the goods aren't delivered endears himself and his organization to the buyer. Sincere good will is more than just living up to the terms of the contract. It involves extra effort—especially when the buyer runs into a snag of some sort. The seller who is there, reliable, and very willing to pitch in and help when a problem crops up, is sooner or later rewarded for his loyalty.

The buyer needs a good explanation. It is important to the buyer that he feels he thoroughly understands your bid, your proposal, your terms and obligations. He needs this understanding for himself and for others in his organization.

The buyer doesn't like to feel he's boxed in. If your company announces a price increase, for example, it is not good for the buyer to get this news from a cold form letter or similar communication. This gives him a feeling that he's pinned against the wall—a feeling that brings resentment. Tell him about the price increase in person and do it with a good explanation of the reasons for the increase.

The buyer wants to be listened to. The more you listen to the buyer's wants, needs, and problems, the better he will like it. And the more you will learn, about him and his organization.

The buyer wants peace of mind. He doesn't want to have to worry about whether you will deliver what you said you will deliver, when you said you would deliver it. He wants to deal with sellers who are stable, dependable.

You've never seen a purchase order that included "one pound of security," "two pounds of reliability," "three pounds of ego," "four pounds of trust," but these and all the other satisfiers are part and parcel of every purchase order ever written.

On the surface these very human wants and needs of the buyer, which figure in every negotiation, have nothing to do with price. Nothing could be further from the truth. They have everything to do with price because they diminish price, they shrink its importance—if the sales person takes the time to help them do it. The more of these wants that are met, the more the buyer will pay.

The buyer raps his fingers on the desk and talks about price, price, price. As the tip of the iceberg, price is ever visible, ever under discussion. The other buyer wants, the "satisfiers," run silently but run deep—making up that larger mass of the iceberg that is unseen.

The trick is to turn the iceberg over—bringing the satisfiers to the surface, making them more visible and important, and pushing price down, making it less visible, less important.

How does the seller do this? With time.

Just as time is the key to so many other aspects of success in negotiation, it is the key to upsetting the iceberg.

The more time the seller devotes to the buyer's other wants, the more the buyer will pay. And the more he will strive to justify his action—to himself and to his organization.

This is why sales people should avoid quickie deals, unless they are very well prepared for them. There is no time to turn the iceberg over in the quickie deal. As a result, the quickie deal is usually characterized by fast price-lowering on the part of the seller, a rapid slide to the bottom line of the price scale.

Inherent in the whole concept of time is the quality of patience—one of the most important characteristics of the successful negotiator.

We in sales are typically not long on patience. We constantly have to remind ourselves of its importance. But we're not alone. Americans generally are impatient, anxious to get on with it, eager to get things over. This is even true in diplomatic circles.

When the North Vietnamese went to Paris to begin the peace talks they leased a villa for two years. They went there prepared to be patient, prepared to use time. I'm sure Averell Harriman and Philip Habib checked in at the Ritz on a day-to-day basis. The Chinese and Russians, too, have demonstrated time and time again how much patience they bring to negotiation. It's part of their culture.

But Americans, and especially Americans in sales, have

to work at being patient, and work hard at it. It just doesn't come naturally to us.

The rule is simple: *In negotiation, patience certainly is a virtue, and a valuable one.*

The use of time in negotiation often takes the form of the deadline. It's used by buyers sometimes as a tactic—a way of taking time away from sellers.

What we sellers must remember is to be skeptical of deadlines, and to best them. Most can be renegotiated.

Our nation's income tax deadline is probably the most famous deadline of our time. But we taxpayers know we can negotiate an extension. When we travel, we see signs in hotels and motels that declare twelve noon checkout time, or one P.M. checkout time. But we who travel a great deal know that these checkout times are negotiable.

Deadlines take time from us, and time—as we have said repeatedly—is our most valuable tool in negotiation. We sellers respond too quickly to time pressures. It's important that we stop and think—and question the time limit.

If a buyer says a bid must be in his hands by a certain date, chances are if you call him and tell him you need more time, you'll get it. Some deadlines are real, immovable. Many can be stretched.

Think before responding when you hear such things as:

- I have to place the order by Wednesday.
- My boss has to approve and he's leaving tomorrow for a week in Europe.
- If we can't agree, I talk to your competitor tomorrow.
- The money for this won't be available after June 30.
- I'll not be responsible for buying this after Friday.
- The fiscal year ends December 3.

- This is my schedule. If you can't meet it, I'll have to go elsewhere.
- The procurement committee meets tomorrow. Do you want the order at that price?

These kinds of deadlines are common in negotiation and we must stay on guard lest they rob us of time.

There are also deadlines that we, the sellers, can use—deadlines designed to get the buyer to buy. They are at our command and we can use them to take time away from the buyer—time which he could use to shop around. Here are some:

- The offer is good for 15 days.
- The price goes up July 1.
- The option expires June 30.
- Inventory is subject to prior sale.
- If we don't have the order by June 1, we can't deliver by June 30.
- It will take eight weeks to get it through our production plant.
- Place the order immediately to ensure availability.
- The cargo ship leaves at two P.M. Do you want space on it?
- If we don't get your deposit tomorrow, we can't hold it.

Deadline is the use of time to force action. On the one hand, we sales people must be on the alert against being pushed into premature action without first testing the deadline. (The more we know about the buyer and his organization and its way of doing business, the better we can judge the validity of a deadline.) On the other hand, we must remember the deadline as a tool to get buyers to act quickly.

The concept of time permeates negotiation. Time to discover and use your powers. Time to discover and counteract buyer tactics. Time for the buyer want to change, and time for you to help his want change. Time to deal with the deadline—and to use the deadline. And: time to make concessions the smart way—the next topic on our agenda.

15

Negotiating to Satisfy

The seller who gets the highest price is always the happiest seller. Right? The buyer who gets the lowest price is always the happiest buyer. Right?

Wrong on both counts.

In negotiation, satisfaction is a tricky thing.

Think about it for a minute. Don't you have a customer who's paying top list price and is perfectly pleased, never bothers you at all? Don't you have another customer who is getting the maximum discount, say 20 percent, yet is constantly complaining, nibbling for extras and freebies? Of course you do.

How come? Is it simply that the first guy is a good guy and the second guy is a bad guy? Not at all. The answer lies in how they got the prices they got.

Remember the 1966 Mustang convertible I bought when I was a kid? Some years later I decided to sell it. The particular model had become increasingly popular with young people, increasingly in demand. I'd taken very good care of it so it was still in beautiful condition.

I decided to sell it, and go for top dollar. I read the newspaper ads for similar cars. They ranged around $2300 to $2500. I decided I'd advertise it for $3500 and settle for $2700.

Some of my friends thought my asking price was too high, much too high. I gave them a lecture. *In negotiation you aim higher and you come out better,* I told them. *You take time. You have patience. I was prepared to wait for the buyer who'd pay my price.*

I called the Los Angeles *Times* and arranged for the ad to run four Sundays. And I started planning what I figured would be a tough negotiation, for top dollar.

Late that Saturday I got a call from a prospective buyer. He'd gotten the early edition of the Sunday *Times,* seen the ad, and wanted to see the car. Could he do it that night? No, I told him, that wasn't possible. But he could come at nine o'clock the next morning.

He showed up at eight-forty-five. He was a quiet, polite fellow. We shook hands, then he began looking over the Mustang. He walked around it, opened the front door and sat in the driver's seat for a minute, got out and opened the hood and looked at the engine for about half a minute. Could he take it for a little drive? I said sure. He got in the car and headed for the town of Westwood, the section of Los Angeles where I was living then.

Seven minutes later he was back. "I really like the car, Gary, and I'd like to take it." As he talked he was pulling his billfold from his pocket. He withdrew a check and handed it to me. It was a bank check, for $3500, made out in my name.

Now, here's the question: How did I feel?

Initially, I felt great. As he drove away I looked at the check and thought: *Terrific. I got top dollar and I got it quickly and easily.*

Then, as I walked up the front steps of my apartment building, it suddenly hit me. What a jerk I'd been! If he paid $3500 that easily, maybe I could have gotten $3750 or even $4000. What a jerk!

That buyer may have been the only person in the world who'd pay $3500 for that Mustang. Maybe even the only one who'd pay $3000. But I didn't think of that. All I thought about was if I got the $3500 that easily, maybe I could have gotten more.

So here's this car buyer. He couldn't have been nicer. He couldn't have been more polite. He took up very little of my time. He didn't question my price—a high price. He just smiled and handed the check to me. And he made me feel lousy.

Negotiation's my business, so I knew what was going on. But if it weren't, what would I have done? Well, eventually, I would have rationalized my jerk feelings and decided I had made a good deal. I would have looked at ads for 1966 Mustangs for several weeks, and seen they were going for $2500, $2600, $2700, and concluded I had indeed gotten a good price.

But that was a one-shot deal. Industrial selling doesn't usually involve many one-shot deals. You call on customers time after time and, you hope, year after year. And how that customer feels about his previous transactions with you has an enormous influence on his current transaction with you.

Suppose that buyer of my 1966 Mustang hadn't made it

so easy for me. Suppose he started out with an offer of $2500, and we went back and forth and, eventually, I got him up to $3000 and we closed the deal.

How would I have felt? I would have felt great. He only wanted to pay $2500 and I got him up to $3000. Good for me. I'd done very well. Yes, I would have felt better with the $3000 than I did with the $3500 that came to me too easily.

Now, what's going on here? What's going on is the concept that, whether you're a buyer or a seller, your feelings of satisfaction may often depend more on how you got the price than they do on the price itself.

Let's take an example in industrial selling.

You're the sales person and you have a product and you're asking $100,000 for it. But times are not that great, you're dealing with a longterm customer, and you and your superiors decide that you'll take $90,000.

I'm the buyer. I get several bids for your kind of product, from you and your competitors, and I go over them with my purchasing director and the engineer for that particular project. We go over them carefully.

The engineer likes yours best. "It's the best designed, it works, it looks like it will be the most durable," he says. "We've got the $100,000 in the budget. Let's give it to him and get the thing and get going."

The purchasing director agrees but, naturally, doesn't want to pay first full price if we don't have to. "Okay," he tells me. "We want the thing. But let's go in with an offer of $95,000. Try that first. And, if you have to, go to $96,000 or $96,500, or even $97,000."

Four weeks have gone by since you gave me your bid. Your boss keeps asking you about it. The support people who helped you with the proposal keep asking you about it. You're anxious.

I call you and arrange a meeting. We get together, we talk about business, then about your product. I say, "We really like your product but we have a tight budget on this project. The best we can do is $95,000. I'm sorry, but $100,000 is just too much for our purse on this one."

Immediately, you reach across my desk and shake my hand, saying, "You have a deal. We can live with that."

How do you feel? Great. You would have taken $90,000, you got $95,000. You feel fine.

How do I feel? Not so good. I go back to my boss after our meeting and he asks me, "Well, what happened?"

I say, "I offered him the $95,000—just like we agreed at our meeting Tuesday."

"And?"

"He took it."

My boss looks kind of strange. He shakes his head. We both think the same thing. If you took the $95,000 so quickly, maybe you would have taken $92,000 or $93,000. It's odd, but true. You gave us a bid, we made you a lower offer, you took it. And how do we feel? We feel we paid too much. We're not happy about the deal.

This was not a one-shot deal, like the selling of the Mustang. You and I have a longterm relationship. You'll be calling on me again, giving me proposals again. But my view of you has changed. The next time you call on me I will look at you and I will think, we paid him too much last time.

Maybe it shouldn't be that way, but that's the way it is. I made you an offer, you took it instantly, and from that time on you're the guy I paid too much.

Now, suppose you had reacted differently when I offered you the $95,000. Suppose you were happy with the offer—after all, you would have taken $90,000. But you didn't make it so easy for me.

Suppose you had said, "Gee, I don't know. We figured this one really closely. Let me think about it and get back to you this afternoon. Let me talk to my boss, and I'll call you later. I just don't know if we can do it for that. We need a little time."

I would have gone to my boss and told him, "Well, I offered him the $95,000 and he's going to talk to his manager and get back to me later. They may take it, or something close to it."

You call me later that day. Maybe you say you and your boss sharpened your pencils and figure you can do it for $96,000. Maybe you say you can do it for $95,000.

Whether you take my offer, or try to get it up just a little, you've made me work just a little harder for the price. I feel better about it. My boss feels better about it. We feel better about you and your company. We think we negotiated well and got a good price, and we're happy.

The next time I see you? I don't think of you as the guy I paid too much. I came away from our transaction happy, and I'm glad to do business with you again.

The point is, in terms of my satisfaction after a deal, how I got the price I paid was more important than the price itself. And how I got the price will affect our relationship from that time on.

When you took my offer so quickly, I immediately felt I was paying too much. And, chances are, I would try to get some of it back in some way. I might push for free training for some of our employees, or I might ask you to pick up the freight charges, or I might want 20 extra manuals, free, or I might ask you to change the terms, delay the payment. And, first thing you know, you're spending time catering to my nibbles that you should be spending out selling.

This kind of thing happens in real estate. Not long ago a building on Wilshire Boulevard in Los Angeles was put on the market for $10 million. The day after it went on the market a buyer appeared at the seller's office with his attorney, prepared to pay the $10 million.

What happened? The seller declined the offer, took the building off the market, raised the price to $15 million, and put it back on the market. He had gotten his asking price too quickly, and figured it couldn't be a good deal. He put a price on the building, he got the price, and he refused it.

If, on the other hand, the buyer had gone in with an offer of $7 million or $8 million, what would have happened? Probably, they would have negotiated, gone through a couple of counteroffers, and settled at $9 million or $9.5 million. And the seller would have felt fine about the deal.

Again, how we get the price is more important to our satisfaction than the price itself.

The point of all this is that we sellers must remember to always say no one more time before we say yes. And it's important in every negotiation: *Always say no one more time before saying yes.*

Here again, we see how important time is in negotiation. We don't scream, "Absolutely not," or "No way." We say we need time to think about the offer, or time to go over our figures again, or time to talk about it to our superiors.

How much time do we take? That's a business judgment. Certainly there's always the risk of not getting the business if we hem and haw too much. How far we can go varies from one situation to another. But whether it's a matter of taking a few minutes to call our home office to check the offer with them, or a day to go over our proposal more carefully, we have made the buyer think he's worked at least a little to get his price. And he feels better about it.

In industrial selling, every negotiation affects every other negotiation. We're negotiating one deal but what happens in that negotiation affects our next negotiation with that buyer, and the next one, and the next one. The buyer feels good about us, and his business with us, or he doesn't feel good about it. And one of the most important factors determining this is how he got the prices he got.

There's another problem with lowering our prices too quickly, taking offers too quickly. It can send the business to one of our competitors. Or, put another way, I can lose a sale because I lowered my price too quickly.

It happens this way. I bid $10,000 on a job. I'm low bidder. But the buyer's doing his job, so he offers me $8000. I take it instantly.

The buyer thinks, gee, if they took that low offer so quickly, maybe one of the other bidders will take an even lower offer. And next thing I know, even though I was low bidder, and immediately went lower, the buyer backs out, dealing with my competitors. Perhaps successfully.

I didn't remember to say no one more time before saying yes, and the buyer began looking elsewhere. I made it too easy for him.

So we have two seeming contradictions that are true. A

buyer may feel far better about a $10 price than he does about a $9 price. A seller can lose a sale by lowering his price.

My job as seller is to leave the buyer happy, feeling good about himself and about the deal. And, regardless of price, if he gets it too quickly and too easily, he doesn't feel that good about himself, and he's not that happy.

As Shakespeare said, "He is well paid who is well satisfied."

The key to this aspect of negotiation is knowing how to make concessions—the smart way. And making concessions the smart way means you end up with more money, your company ends up with more profit, and you end up with a happier buyer.

16

Making Concessions

In negotiation, how you concede can be more important than what you concede. In fact, concession can bring you closer to the deal or farther away—depending on how you do it.

Remember my story about the sales person with the word processing system I had made up my mind to buy? He lowered his price so much and so quickly and so often that I began to wonder if there was some problem with his company, or his product, and I started looking at competitive systems.

Several years ago, there was a big hotel project, in a midwestern city. A $100 million project. The developers had all the land they needed except for one little corner. An elderly widow owned a little house on this corner, and she said she didn't want to sell.

The developers called in their attorneys. "We've got the financing for the project," they told the lawyers. "We've got the money. The architects are ready to go. The contractors are ready to go. Go buy that little house—get it done."

The attorneys meet with the widow. They offer her $400,000 for her property—a very high price.

She thinks for awhile. Then: "I don't think so," she says. "This is my home. I've lived here for 40 years. I don't really want to sell it. I don't really want to move."

The attorneys leave. A week later they go back. They offer her $600,000. The elderly widow is sweet and polite. But she turns them down.

The developers give the attorneys hell. *Buy the damn house,* they tell them. *Get it done. Let's get on with this project.*

The lawyers raise their offer to $800,000. Still no sale.

The widow calls her friend Mabel. "Gee, Mabel, every time I see these people they go up another two hundred grand."

"Great," says Mabel. "Have them over more often."

A month goes by. What's going on? The lawyers are up to $1.4 million with the offer. The widow's still there, waiting for a $1.6 million offer.

Now, suppose the lawyers had handled it differently. Suppose they had started with the $400,000, then on the second offer went to $450,000, and on the third to $470,000, and on the fourth to $480,000, and on the next one, $483,000. Messages go back and forth in negotiation. And if they'd done it that way, she would have gotten the message that they were obviously going up less each time— and that she had gone just about as far as she could go.

That story illustrates one guideline to smart concession-making: *Concede in small increments and, when possible, diminishing increments. Give in a little at a time.*

If I, the sales person, make a big concession every time

I see my customer, the buyer, it would be just like the widow and her friend Mabel. The buyer says to his boss, "Gee, every time I see Gary, I get a big concession." And his boss says, "Great, see him more often."

So, giving in a little at a time makes very good sense in negotiation.

Here's another guideline to concession-making: *Give in slowly*. And I have a story from my own experience about this one.

A few years ago I was looking at space in a small office building in west Los Angeles. I'd looked at the space twice and decided I wanted some things done before getting into the price per square foot. I had a list of ten things I wanted done. I sat down across the desk from the manager, a small, elderly woman. After a few minutes' conversation I got into my list.

"I'd like the three outer offices painted," I said.

"I see." She looked at me thoughtfully for a few moments. She started writing on a pad. She turned to a little calculator for a time. Then she wrote some more on the pad. She got up and went to a filing cabinet, pulled out a file folder, and looked at the pages inside it. By this time 14 or 15 minutes had elapsed. She returned to her chair and looked at me.

"All right. I guess we can paint the offices."

I moved on to number two on my list. "I'd like to have maintenance—janitorial service—five days a week instead of three days."

"Oh," she said. She went through the pad and calculator again. Then she looked up. "Excuse me. I'll have to talk to the people in maintenance." She got up and walked to the back, through a door to another office.

I sat there looking around. I picked up an old magazine that I'd already read and looked at it again. I put it down and looked around some more. I thought I should be at work. I thought about all I had to do that day. Fifteen minutes went by, then 18 minutes. Then 20 minutes. Finally she came back through the door and sat down at her desk.

"Yes. I talked to maintenance and I guess we can do the service five days a week."

What do you think I did with the rest of my list with the eight other things on it? I crumpled it up and threw it away and signed up to lease the offices.

She had made me work so hard and wait so long for each little concession, she wore me down. I would have been there all day. And I think she knew exactly what she was doing. I think she knew all along she could have the three offices painted, and provide janitorial services five days a week.

For all I knew she could have been writing a letter to her daughter in Duluth on that pad, while I cooled my heels. Or figuring her income tax. Or making her grocery list and calculating how much she'd need to go to the supermarket.

Somewhere this woman had learned that time is money in negotiation. Somewhere she had learned about the *considered response*—one of the important concepts in concession-making.

We're told the good sales person has all the answers on the tip of his tongue. He knows his company, he knows his product, he knows his service, he knows what he can do and can't do, he speaks with authority, he makes decisions quickly. But is that always smart?

Let's suppose I was dealing with a hotshot real estate broker that day. I asked for the office painting and he immediately said, "No problem." I asked for the five-day service, and he instantly replied, "You got it."

I would have gone through the ten things on my list in five minutes—and along the way I probably would have thought up two or three more things to ask for.

What does this tell us? Sometimes it pays not to be so decisive, not to be so fast with the answers, not to be so alertly responsive.

This idea, of giving in slowly—the considered response—is especially important for the seller who deals in a fixed-price product.

Sometimes a sales person attending my seminar will raise his hand and say, "I have a fixed-price product. I don't negotiate."

That's wrong. Even when dealing in fixed-price products, we negotiate. We negotiate terms, or delivery, or freight cost, or installation, or training, or tie-in advertising, or any one of many other things involved in many negotiations.

Still, if we cannot negotiate price, we have to produce as much satisfaction as we can in the buyer from those things we can negotiate. And we don't make that buyer satisfied by snapping immediately, "You got it," or "No problem."

We try to make the buyer earn the concession, if only just a little. We hesitate, ask for time to think, ask for time to call the boss, or say we'll get back to the buyer.

Then the buyer will feel better. And he can go to his boss and say, "I couldn't get the price down. It's fixed. But I got delivery in two weeks instead of four, and ten free manuals." Or whatever.

Another concession-making guideline: *Give yourself room to negotiate.*

Inherent in this guideline is the concept of aiming higher, which we've discussed. Aim higher, you come out better. You'll recall that we demonstrated how practical experience as well as research in negotiation proved that this is true.

Giving yourself room to negotiate—aiming higher— means giving yourself more room to make concessions, concessions that don't eat away at your company's profit. But there are some things we must remember when we go in high—and they're important.

First, we should always give reasons for our proposal, why the price is what it is. Buyers like and need explanations with proposals. They like explanations themselves and they are able to pass on the explanations to their bosses.

Second, we should never come up with a high proposal, cross our fingers, throw it over the fence, and run for cover.

We can't give reasons or explanations when we do it this way. And we can give the buyer the notion the high price is not negotiable, when we don't want to.

The proposal, and especially the high one, must be followed up. We should call on the customer, in person or by phone, within a few days after submitting it. And call a few days after that. And a few days after that. If we don't do that, the buyer may just look at the high proposal and say to himself, "This guy just doesn't care whether he gets the business or not," and go on to other bids.

Don't think you must give tit for tat. This guideline is an important one, and covers something we've all done.

Consider the case where we bid a price of $90, the buyer offers $70, and there we stand. If the buyer then goes up to $75, does that mean we must go down to $85? Does it mean we must give tit for tat? Certainly not. Nowhere is it written that our concession must be an amount equal to the buyer's concession. If the buyer goes from $70 to $75, there's no reason in the world why we can't go down from $90 to $89 or $88. There's no reason in the world why we should think we have to give tit for tat.

Related to the idea of not giving tit for tat is that of not splitting the difference. If the buyer says to us, "Let's split the difference," our tendency is to go along with that.

But splitting the difference means what? That you get half, that you get 50 percent. Why not go for 70 percent or 60 percent? We don't have to feel compelled to split the difference just because someone suggests it. We can say, "Well, we can't really do that, we can't really split the difference. It's too close. We can go 30 percent, but not 50."

Another guideline: *Don't mishandle the ridiculous offer.*

I remember something that happened when I was younger and working in sales for a subcontractor in the construction industry. He was asked to make a bid on a job; he figured he could do it for about $90,000 and bid $100,000. He worked hard on his proposal, driving 40 miles to present it and go over it with the prospective customer.

The customer looked it over and told my boss: "That's ridiculous. I can get it done for $50,000. Your price is insane."

My boss felt he'd been taken advantage of. He felt he'd been manipulated. He got angry. He said to the prospect, "Well go get it done for $50,000," and grabbed his proposal back and stormed out.

A year later I ran into the subcontractor who had gotten that project and completed it. I asked him how much he had been paid for it. The subcontractor replied, "It was $90,000."

That buyer had known his figure of $50,000 was ridiculous. But he also figured why not try it anyway, why not test the water?

When we put in a proposal and the buyer comes back with an offer like that, one that is ridiculously low, what do we do? Too often, we react the way my boss did in that case. We think, gee, I worked hard on that proposal, my manager went over it carefully, my support people helped me with it. This buyer just made a fool of me. We want to tell the buyer to forget it or to shove it and we want to storm out. And too often we do that, or something like that.

The way to handle the ridiculous offer is calmly and politely, and in such a way that you leave the door open for future negotiation. The reason is that the buyer may well think his offer is as silly as you do, but he's taking a flyer.

Let's say your unit price is $10 and the buyer likes the product and figures he'll end up paying $8 or maybe even $9. But he says to himself, what the hell, it can't hurt, I'll offer him $5 and see if he goes for it.

He's taking a longshot. He figures if you turn it down he hasn't lost anything. He can still negotiate. But he can't negotiate if you slam the door closed.

When this happens, I try to remember to say something like this: "I appreciate your offer, and we want your business. But we're just too far apart. We're not even on the same ballfield. But I'd like to ask you to think about it some more. And I'll call you next Tuesday. I would really like your business and hope you take another look at our proposal and change your mind."

This way, I'm walking away from the offer but I'm leaving the door open for more realistic negotiation.

Walking away this way, instead of storming away in anger, I keep hostility out of the negotiation. Hostility has no place in longterm business negotiation, whatever the circumstances. It clouds our thinking, distorts our intelligence with emotion, cripples our negotiating skill.

Planning ahead is important for any negotiation and one of the most critical things to plan is how we'll react if we get a ridiculous offer. If we plan that reaction, we'll react calmly, and in a way that doesn't blow the business forever.

Another important concession-making guideline: *Don't be the first to concede on major issues.*

Being the first to concede on minor issues is okay, sometimes a good idea. You don't give up much, you show you're agreeable to bargaining, you get the negotiating going.

But being the first to concede on a major issue tends to put us at a disadvantage. It makes us look like we're too eager to lower our price, or make whatever the major concession may be. If, on the other hand, we're first to concede on a minor issue, the buyer can be first to concede on a major issue and still save face.

One more guideline: *Beware of conceding too much as the deadline nears.*

Dr. Karrass's experiment, which we've discussed several times, demonstrated that negotiators tend to make larger concessions as the deadline nears. Unskilled negotiators made much larger concessions than they'd made earlier. Even skilled negotiators made somewhat larger concessions as time ran out.

This is why being skeptical about deadlines, and testing whenever possible to see if the deadline is a real one, is so important.

Has this ever happened to you? The buyer says he has to have your best price by three o'clock Friday. A month later, you're still negotiating. That three o'clock Friday wasn't really a deadline. Or, at least, it wasn't a very important one.

The point is, try to be sure a deadline is real before you regard it as such. And remember: the time to watch your concession pattern closely is that time approaching the deadline. We all must beware of the tendency to concede too much when the deadline nears.

There's another side to this coin. If the buyer is running out of inventory, or under some other deadline pressure to place the order—and they often are—chances are he will make larger concessions than earlier in the negotiation. It's to the seller's advantage to stretch out the time of the negotiation, moving that buyer closer and closer to his deadline. He'll give more.

To sum up:

- The buyer's satisfaction often depends more on how he got the price than it does on the price itself. He can feel better about a $10 price that he feels he negotiated than a $9 price that came too easily.
- How you concede can be more important than what you concede.
- Concede in small increments and, when possible, diminishing increments. Give in a little at a time.

- Give in slowly.
- Give yourself room to negotiate.
- Don't think you must give tit for tat, or split the difference.
- Don't mishandle the ridiculous offer.
- Don't be first to concede on major issues.
- Watch out for conceding too much at deadline time.

The overall concept to remember about concession-making is that we want to wring as much buyer satisfaction as possible out of each concession. And, since none of us overly values things that come too easily, we want the buyer to figure he earned that concession in some way. He'll feel better about the deal. And about us.

17

What's a Bargain?

What else gives a buyer satisfaction?

We've talked about basic human wants and needs that are "satisfiers," and about making concessions the smart way—so that they give the buyer satisfaction. There's another important thing that contributes to buyer satisfaction: the bargain.

Everyone loves a bargain. If the buyer feels he got a bargain he will be more satisfied, he will look forward to dealing with the sales person again.

But do we really understand just what a bargain is?

We sellers look upon the bargain as purely a matter of price. Full price, no bargain. Less than full price, somewhat of a bargain. Substantially less than full price, a real bargain. Or, so we think.

But this is, to say the least, a very limited view of the bargain.

There are a number of things—circumstances, conditions, facts—that give us the feeling we got a bargain. Some have to do with price. Some don't.

One example:

You sell a certain kind of machine. I want one, but I want last year's model because it's a little cheaper and I don't need the new features of the new model.

You say to me, "We had one left, but I think it's sold. I'll check it out and get back to you."

Two days later you call. "I was right. The last one was sold. But the customer had trouble with the financing, so it's loose again and available. It's yours."

I feel great. I feel like I got a bargain. Why? Because it's a little cheaper than the new model? No. I knew that, I expected that. I feel like I got a bargain for two other reasons:

1. I got something somebody else wanted.
2. I got the last one.

Both of these conditions, which have nothing to do with price, give me the feeling I got a bargain.

Here's another one. If I pay less than the established price, I get the feeling of the bargain. And this is where the power of legitimacy—in the form of the printed price list—comes in handy.

Suppose your printed price sheet lists 13 cents a pound for your product, in quantities of 1000 pounds and more. We negotiate, and we conclude at a price of 11 cents a pound. Of course, I get the feeling of the bargain.

It might be that not one of your customers pays the full price of 13 cents a pound. It might be that most of them only pay ten cents a pound.

But I don't know that. I know the sheet says 13 cents and I paid 11 cents. So I get the feeling of the bargain. As a matter of fact, I probably assume other customers are paying more than I am. That gives me the feeling of the bargain, too.

Suppose the price I pay is a good deal less than the price I thought I would have to pay. That will give me the feel of the bargain. Even if my idea of the price I'd pay was way off, much too high, I'll still get the feeling of the bargain if I pay less.

Other conditions that suggest a bargain?

1. *If there's a very low risk of my being dissatisfied, or having trouble or hassle with the product in the long run.* The product may be expensive, but if I know from experience that I and my co-workers will be well satisfied with it, will have minimum or no trouble with it, and will get prompt attention if it does become troublesome, I'll look upon the price as well worth it, as a bargain, even if the price is expensive.

2. *If the product becomes evidence that I have good taste.* I may pay top dollar to redecorate and re-furnish my offices, then start worrying that I paid too much. But if visitors rave about how wonderful it looks, how functionally it's arranged, my feelings change. Because the work becomes evidence of my good taste and judgment, I begin to feel it was a kind of bargain.

3. *If I'm told by others that I got a bargain.* I may be dealing in a product arena that I'm not familiar with. I may not know whether the price I paid was high or average or low. But if others tell me it was a bargain, I feel I got a bargain.

4. *If the price is good in terms of the performance received per dollar.* If I know your product will be more efficient, more dependable, and last twice as long as the competitive product, I'll pay your price and get the feeling of a bargain, even if your price is substantially higher. It's the idea of the bang for the buck. If I know the $100 pair of shoes will last twice as long as the $65 shoes, I'll buy the more expensive ones, and feel I got a bargain.

5. *If something else is thrown in.* Remember my friend who always asked for a free tie whenever he bought a suit? He may have paid $200 for a suit that wasn't really worth $200. But if the haberdasher threw in the free tie, he figured he got a bargain. We see this in supermarkets. The maker of the detergent glues a wash cloth on the side of the box and we pay no attention to the price of the detergent. We're getting a free wash cloth if we buy the detergent, so we think we're getting a bargain.

At some point during every negotiation we sellers should ask ourselves: Is there something I can do to help this buyer get the feeling he got a bargain? That feeling will, of course, contribute to his general satisfaction with the deal. And that satisfaction is the key to future business.

18

What's a Lousy Penny?

When I'm spending cash I shop carefully, check out prices carefully, count out money carefully. When I'm using my MasterCard, I turn into a minor league J. Paul Getty, barely glancing at prices, spending more and more easily. Even when I'm paying by check instead of cash, I spend more.

Why? Credit cards and checks are funny money.

Last time I was in Las Vegas I bet $50 in chips on a roll of the dice and lost. Later I told myself I had no business betting $50 on a roll of the dice. Was I crazy? Why did I do it? I did it because $50 is a very small pile of chips. It didn't seem like I was betting much. And that's why they use chips in casinos. They're funny money and people gamble more loosely with them than they would with cash.

Have you ever noticed that many used car dealers, land developers, and even retail stores advertise their products in terms of instalment payments instead of the full price?

They know we'll consider $50 a month or $100 a month or $300 a month a lot quicker than we'll consider a full price of $1000 or $5000 or $15,000. Why? Instalment payments are funny money.

Not long ago a friend of mine was negotiating to buy a house for $160,000. Before the deal closed the bank raised its interest rate from 11 to 11½ percent. What was his reaction? He said, "Oh, what's the difference, 11 or 11½ percent." If he had taken the time to calculate what the half percent meant in dollars over the life of the 30-year mortgage, he would have sung a different tune.

But he didn't—because interest is funny money.

To close an order, have you negotiated free customer training, free service, free transportation, special delivery, tax, freight, longer payment terms? Then you've negotiated funny money.

And the point about funny money is this: it must be watched very carefully. It must be negotiated very carefully. It must be thoroughly thought out and—most important—it must be translated into real dollars or some other sort of real value.

Even the unit price of your product can be funny money if you don't think of it the right way. The right way means in terms of the total.

Here's an example:

You're the seller and I'm the buyer. We're negotiating an order for 2 million pounds of one of the chemicals you sell.

Your asking price is 20 cents a pound. I offer you 19 cents a pound. I lean on you. I say, "Come on—what's a lousy penny?"

If you only think in terms of 20 cents a pound, and 19

cents a pound, and the "lousy penny," you're negotiating funny money.

Suppose, on the other hand, you think this way:

The 2 million pounds at 20 cents a pound comes to $400,000. Of this, $60,000 would be profit.

The 2 million pounds at 19 cents a pound comes to $380,000. Of this, $40,000 would be profit.

This means, of course, that if you take the 19 cents—if you forget the "lousy penny"—you lose $20,000 -and it's all profit.

If you negotiate with that $20,000 in mind, instead of the penny or the 19 cents or the 20 cents, will you negotiate differently? Will you try harder to get your price? You sure will.

You have translated the funny money into real money. And whenever we do this, it has a profound effect on how we negotiate.

You had two choices. You could think about giving up a penny a pound, or you could think about giving up $20,000 profit. Arithmetic tells us they're the same. But anyone who has ever negotiated knows they're not. They're very different.

Whatever your unit price—pennies a pound, dollars a pound, $100 each, dollars an hour, dollars per thousand—you're negotiating in funny money if you don't think in terms of the total involved in the negotiation.

Can a million dollars be funny money? It certainly can.

I have a friend who is with a very large corporation, one that grosses more than $12 billion yearly. Major policy decisions of this corporation are made by the board of directors. Major operational decisions are made by an executive management committee.

He sat in on a meeting of the executive management committee. This is how he tells about it:

"The meeting went on all morning and most of the afternoon. The committee made decisions involving many millions of dollars. There were capital investment projects, involving new plants and additions to old existing plants—the projects ranged from $14 million to $40 million.

"They approved manufacturing division projects involving many millions, and marketing plans involving millions.

"One guy who came in to make his pitch was from the company's smallest division. It markets educational materials to junior colleges.

"He outlined a plan to expand his division's market, geographically. It was a thorough plan, for a yearlong marketing thrust into the new area. When he concluded he said he estimated the new marketing program would add $1 million to his division's gross revenues for the year.

"One of the members of the management committee looked at this guy, then said, 'The plan's okay. But do you really want to go to all that trouble for a million dollars?' "

Well, that executive had been dealing in many millions all day. One million had little meaning for him. He forgot what a million dollars is.

We all do that. If you're negotiating something that involves many thousands of dollars, does another one thousand one way or the other mean much? No. What if you're negotiating something that involves hundreds of dollars? What does one thousand dollars mean then? A great deal.

Even real money can be funny money if we don't keep its real value in perspective.

That's the big thing about negotiating any kind of funny money—keeping the real value in mind.

In our business we had trouble with our computer sys-

tem, which is new. The first time it happened the salesman sent over two service people and they worked for
days getting it straight. He did this gratis.

Some months later, we had trouble again. He sent a
service man again, and he corrected the problem. But
several days later I got a bill. The bill showed 12 hours of
service at $39 an hour, and there was the total—$468. But
the bill was marked, "No charge," and initialed by the
salesman.

He had negotiated funny money—free service. But he
had also put his focus, and mine, on the real value. And
the free service meant a great deal more to me that time
than it had meant the first time.

There's a lot of funny money in real estate transactions,
besides the bank's interest rate. Financial institutions
charge what they call points. If one charges two points and
another charges two and a half points, there doesn't seem
to be much difference, on the surface. But points are
money. If it's a $10 million deal, a point is $100,000 and a
point and a half, of course, is $150,000.

Real estate agency commission is another kind of real
estate funny money. The difference between six and six
and a half percent commission—that little half percent—
can be a sizable sum in a commercial real estate transaction. The Rothschilds got wealthy on one-eighth of a percent.

Many large corporations got wise some years ago to the
fact that they were giving funny money away to employees and not really getting credit for it. So they started
explaining, in dollars and cents, how much the life insur-
ance and medical and dental plans cost, how much they
meant to the individual employee, in real money.

The same was true in executive hiring. If a company

offered an executive $65,000 plus a company car, plus life insurance, plus medical and dental plans, he walked out saying to himself, "They offered me $65,000."

Many companies rephrased their offers, describing them as "compensation packages." They put a dollar value on the benefits and described the offer not as $65,000 plus this and that, but as a compensation package valued at $80,000—or whatever it all added up to.

In negotiation, one of the problems with funny money is that when we concede it—in the form of free service, or supplies or transportation, or whatever—we don't get much credit for the concession, don't get much buyer satisfaction, unless we translate the concession into real value.

One sales person who attended our seminar dealt in aircraft that cost about $1 million. He could give a customer a six percent discount—$60,000.

"If I offered a six percent discount," he told us, "the customer would be inclined to push for seven or eight percent. Even if I offered $60,000, it didn't seem like a big discount on a million-dollar product. So I say this: I can give you two free trips to Paris and 12 months' maintenance, free of charge. That seems to work better."

There's a case where the most impressive real value of the concession was not the cash but another form of real value.

The rule is: When conceding funny money, try to get as much buyer satisfaction as you can out of the concession.

A two percent discount may mean absolutely nothing to the customer. Two months' free supplies may mean much more.

If you're going to concede funny money, plan ahead. Plan your translation so you can make the concession in terms that have the most real value for that particular customer.

IV

Building Profitable Deals That Stick

19

A Better Deal for Both Parties

Not long ago a businessman from Japan attended one of our negotiation seminars. I had a drink with him the second night, at the end of the seminar, and he said this:

"You know, Americans look upon negotiation as hunting. In Japan, we look upon it as farming.

"I figure there are only so many people out there I can sell to, only so many who will buy from me. So my goal is to take time and care with each negotiation. I want to get the best deal for me and I want the best deal for the customer. I want to farm the relationship.

"Americans want to get in there, get the deal, and get out—the hunting approach. I want to gather harvest from the customer relationship time and time again. And I want to do well each time. But I want the customer to also do well each time. I'm willing to spend the time and effort to achieve this."

He was talking about what we call a better deal for both

parties, something that should be the goal of every negotiation.

The better deal for both parties doesn't just happen. It never just happens. You have to build it. You have to make it happen. How? By always asking for something in return.

Sounds simple, and almost contradictory. But it's true. The path to the better deal for both parties is always asking for something in return.

What do you ask for in return? There are a lot of things. Here are some:

VOLUME

"I can lower the unit price from $725 to $695 if you take 200 instead of 100."

"We can live with 11 cents a pound for the chemical instead of 12 cents if you contract for a million pounds instead of 600,000 pounds."

"We can provide the service for $300 a month per location, rather than our quoted price of $374, if you include your locations in Nevada as well as those in California."

LONGER COMMITMENT

"We'll accept your figure if you make it a two-year contract instead of a one-year contract."

"I'll take five and a half percent instead of six percent commission on this real estate transaction if you agree to give me your next two listings."

"We can give you the additional five percent discount if you agree to a minimum reorder in the same quantity."

"Make it a 13-month agreement instead of 12, and we'll shave the four percent from the monthly price." (Going from 12 months to 13 months can have interesting side effects. You can throw the customer off his buying cycle, which is to your advantage, and you can catch the competition off balance.)

ADDITIONAL ITEMS

"We can cut $3 from the gross price of the cups if you can take an equal number of saucers."

"I can give you the other five percent off if you take the grapefruit juice as well as the orange juice."

"If you agree to buy all your supplies for the system from us, we can reduce the system price by $120."

"Take the service contract for 24 months and we can handle the four percent discount on the machine."

"Give us the order for the 9-by-12 envelopes as well as the letter-sized stationery and we'll take your offer of eight percent less."

"Let us maintain your executive cars as well as your delivery trucks and we can cut the monthly charge by ten percent."

"Let us handle some of your residential listings as well as the commercial listings and we'll take the five and a half percent commission."

BETTER TERMS

"If we ship C.O.D. we can live with another four percent discount."

"We can take your offer if you make it net 20 instead of net 30."

"If you agree to pay half now and half on delivery, we can go to the lower price."

"Make it 30-day pay instead of 60-day pay and we can go from the $100,000 to $98,000."

"For tax reasons, it's to our advantage if you delay payment. Put off payment until January, then pay it in full, and we'll cut five percent from the bill."

FREIGHT AND DELIVERY

"Okay, you pick up the cost of the freight and we'll agree to the $4 reduction per unit."

"Our price for the staplers is $2 each, but it costs us about four cents each to ship them. You have trucks going by our plant every week. You pick up the shipment and we'll agree to your offer of $1.95 each."

"Let us put off delivery for six weeks, instead of the usual two weeks, and we'll settle for the lower price."

"We'll give you that discount if we can deliver half now and half in June and July. That way we can keep our people all employed during the two slow months."

"If we can deliver all 200,000 pounds of the chemical at once, and you store it, instead of our delivering 20,000 pounds a month for ten months, we can go down another penny on the price per pound."

REFERRAL

"You have offices in the Midwest. I'll agree to the price you offer, which is about a nine percent discount, if you can arrange for our representative to make a presentation to your counterpart in the midwestern headquarters. Get our guy half an hour with your guy there, and you got the price you want."

PACKAGING

"We'll go for the lower price you offer if we can package them differently. If we can pack 144 to the carton, instead of boxes of a dozen each, you've got the discount."

"If we can deliver the units protected by corrugated but not packed, not boxed, we can cut about three percent from the price."

REVISED SPECIFICATIONS

"If you can take the jars without the blue line around the top, we can lower the price by five percent."

"If we can eliminate this one little feature on the system, then we can accept your offer of $4500."

"Forget about the company insignia on the side of the

glasses, and we can give you the discount you want."

"This model is $375. You're asking if we'll take $325 each. We can't do that. But we have this other model—it has all the same capabilities except the remote one. That one we can give you for $325."

"You're interested in the wall cabinets for their function. If we can deliver them without the glass doors and fancy trim, then we can give you a price that's $30 a unit cheaper."

"Your specs call for lacquer. That's only for appearance and you'll be using them back in the factory. If we can ship them without lacquer, I can give you a better price."

"If you'll just be using them here, you may not need the carrying cases. If we can bid them without the cases, we can do much better on price."

As you see, asking for something in return is the way to build the better deal for both parties. In all the instances above, the buyer is getting a better deal because he's getting a lower price. But the seller is getting a better deal as well because he isn't just lowering his price, he's getting some kind of concession from the buyer, a concession that translates into money.

One of the important things about asking something in return when agreeing to lower a price is that you're not really lowering the plateau of negotiation.

For example, if I'm asking a price of $1 and you're offering 90 cents and I agree to the 90 cents without asking anything in return, the $1 price is gone forever. We never see it or hear it again. The new plateau is 90 cents.

If, on the other hand, I agree to 90 cents only if you pick up the transportation cost, we are still at the $1 plateau—unless you agree to pick up that cost. If you don't go for the transportation item, then we're still at $1 when we begin the next round of negotiation.

Another important aspect of asking for something in return is that you make discoveries, including what the buyer really needs, as opposed to what he may be asking for.

Suppose a buyer calls you in and holds up a glass and says, "Give us a quote on ten gross of these glasses."

Let's say it's a six-ounce glass with a thin decorative line around the top and a design embossed on the side. Your production people aren't set up to produce that kind of glass—unless it's a special custom order. If it's a special custom order, your price is going to be high. You won't get the business.

Maybe the buyer means he needs that exact glass. Maybe he just needs a glass that will fill the need, and someone happened to give him that particular one as an example.

Maybe you say this: "If you can get along without the design embossed on the side, and without the line around the top, we can give you a very good price." And you give him a very good price.

There's a good chance the buyer will say, "Okay, fine. That kind of glass will do."

You have discovered what the buyer really needed, and it was different from what he said he needed.

Because you asked for something in return—in this case, a change in specifications—it became a better deal for both parties.

There are other ways you make discoveries if you ask for something in return.

Let's say the buyer asks for a discount and you say, "Okay, if we can deliver in four weeks instead of two weeks."

The buyer says, "No way. We have to have this stuff within two weeks—sooner if possible."

Does that tell you something? It tells you the buyer is short on time, and probably is not going to use any of it shopping around among your competitors.

Another example. Suppose you tell the buyer he can have his price if you eliminate a certain little feature. He says, "No, don't take that off. That's what our engineers love about your product."

What does this tell you? You may well be the only vendor offering that particular feature. You may be virtually a sole-source vendor.

There's another advantage to always asking something in return. It often helps you in negotiating within your own organization. And one of the most important traits of the skilled negotiator is his ability to negotiate within his own organization.

When you ask for prompt payment in return for a price cut, you're endearing yourself to your accounting people. If you agree to a price cut if you can deliver in a month instead of a week, you're making a better friend of your delivery organization. When you ask for a simpler specification in return for a discount, you're making life a little easier for your production people. And when those times come when you need a special favor—from accounting, or production, or shipping—you'll stand a much better chance of getting it.

Asking for something in return not only builds a better deal for both parties, but has those other side benefits as well.

And there's always some way to build a better deal for both parties.

A friend of mine was shopping for a house, a house with a pool. He found the perfect house for his family. But it didn't have a pool. He couldn't afford to put up the down payment for the house and then put up the money to build a pool.

The seller built the pool, and added the $12,000 cost of the pool to his asking price for the house. That way my friend got his house and his pool—with the cost of the pool amortized over the 30-year life of the mortgage.

It was a better deal for both parties.

Asking for something in return should be one of our cardinal rules in negotiation. But it's one of the things we often forget.

How do you remember? You make a list. You make a general list of the ten or 15 things you can ask for in return when lowering a price or making some other concession. Then, before each negotiation, you look at the general list and pick out the four or five things you can ask for in return in the particular session coming up.

The better deal for both parties, which you build by asking something in return, is especially important in the longterm relationship. And the longterm relationship is especially important in industrial selling.

We don't want to go in, make a killing, and get out. We don't want to hunt. Like the Japanese businessman, we want to farm the relationship. We want to do well in each negotiation, and we want our customer to do well in each negotiation. We want to go back to that customer. We want him to come back to us. The negotiation that concludes with the better deal for both parties is the best negotiation.

20

The Longterm Relationship—
from Both Sides

In our business we do a lot of printing. For some years we used the same printing firm. It was a classic long-term relationship.

I remember well our first meeting with the salesman. His prices were competitive. His samples indicated his company's quality was high. Then we talked about service.

"We need fast turnaround," I said. "From the copy to the finished job—we have to do that in a two-week cycle."

"No problem," he said.

"When we give you the copy we need the type within two days. We make corrections and we need the corrected type within a day."

"No problem," he said.

"We expect the page proofs within two days, and the job completed within a week."

"You got it," he said.

He couldn't have been more attentive. We'd call for copy pickup and he'd be there in half an hour to get it. The type came back on time, we did our correcting, he picked up our corrections at a moment's notice, and next day returned with the new type. The page proofs, the final printing—all went smoothly for some months.

Along about the middle of the first year, things began to take a little longer. One day became two days; two days stretched to three and four days; a week became ten days. Then one afternoon the salesman was too busy to pick up our corrections. Could we have one of our people drop them off? Okay.

Gradually, the salesman became scarcer and scarcer. We found ourselves dealing with his production people. They didn't say "No problem," or "You got it." They came up with problems—reasons why they couldn't do this or that, or why it would take longer, and cost more. Matter of fact, we began to get the impression we were a nuisance to them.

Our bills slowly got higher and higher. Routine services became special in the eyes of the production people. That meant extra charges. Overtime came into the billing picture. That meant extra charges.

The service went down, the costs went up, but we continued doing business with them. Why? It was easy. They did our jobs and they did them satisfactorily in terms of quality. Finding a new printer, explaining our needs, starting, as it were, from scratch, seemed too much of a hassle. So we put it off and put it off—for seven years.

Finally, we changed. And at this writing we're beginning to see signs of the same cycle—the cycle of the long-term relationship.

The sales person's problem is selling. When he makes a sale, it presents an opportunity. But his opportunity becomes a problem to the people in his organization.

He sells and it means the bookkeeper has to send out more bills. The production people have to produce more. The delivery people have to deliver more. His success is a nuisance to them—just another problem for them to deal with.

In the beginning the sales person pays a great deal of attention to his customer. Then, as orders just kind of come in, he pays less and less attention. It's not entirely his fault. His manager is saying, "You got *them*—go out and get new ones." So off he goes. And his relationship with the old customer, his longterm relationship, suffers.

The old customer may hang in there—for years. But it doesn't necessarily mean he's happy. He just hasn't gotten around to confronting the task of finding a new vendor.

It's like the longterm marriage. You can't judge it by its cover. The couple married for 20 years may be happily married. Or they may not. It may last simply because neither partner has gotten around to doing anything about it.

The longterm relationship is tricky. Whether we're on the inside or the outside, we sellers tend to make assumptions that don't hold water.

The seller on the inside may take it for granted that the orders will just keep flowing in, even though he pays virtually no attention to the customer. He may take it for granted he'll always get the business. The seller on the outside may make an equally erroneous assumption—that he'll never get the business.

The longterm relationship, however long it may be, can come to an end very abruptly. The usual cause of death?

Neglect. The sometimes cause? A smart, competitive sales person who doesn't assume he can't get the business; who assumes, in fact, quite the opposite.

If we look at the longterm relationship, we can't help but conclude that it usually benefits the seller more than the buyer. For a number of reasons.

Assuming the seller's product fits the need, and the seller is reliable, it becomes very easy for the buyer to continue to do business with him. It takes little time. It's convenient. The risk factor is low, making it a safe harbor for the buyer. So he keeps coming back.

Other sellers figure the business is locked up; they usually don't even bother to call on the customer. The salesman with the business usually has a clear field.

The longer the longterm relationship, the more the seller learns about the buyer's organization, at every level. This is, of course, to his advantage. The buyer, on the other hand, is usually deskbound. He doesn't learn much about the seller's organization no matter how long he does business with him. This puts him at a disadvantage.

The longer the longterm relationship, the more dependent the buyer becomes on the seller. Ordering is quick and easy, no explanations are necessary. When there's a change, the seller can accommodate the change easily. Requisitions come to the buyer later and later, orders go to the seller later and later. Still, the seller's organization can handle them, simply because they've done it so many times before.

As the buyer becomes more dependent, the seller becomes more complacent, more sloppy—and less attentive. The orders just come in, regularly, so why worry? He makes fewer personal calls, fewer telephone calls. He devotes more and more of his attention to new customers, customers he's still not sure of.

Then one day the seller gets a call from the longtermer, or makes a call, and there's a new buyer on the scene. Or the same buyer with a new memo from his management, reminding him about the element of business called competition. It's a whole new ball game and the seller finds himself caught off base, with his service down and his prices up. Maybe he is able to pick up the pieces. But maybe he isn't, and the longterm relationship is cut short.

Most of us have gone through this. And we didn't have to ask ourselves where we'd gone wrong. It was very plain. We'd neglected the longterm relationship. We paid less and less attention to the customer who, by any logic, deserved more and more attention.

We forgot about the power of wooing—the key to not only preserving but strengthening the longterm relationship.

We forgot to treat the old customer as well as we treat the new customer.

The longterm relationship demands and deserves *more* of our attention, not less. It must be constantly nourished or it may gradually wither, and die. It must be constantly nourished or it will be vulnerable to attack—from the competition.

The fact that a longterm relationship has lasted a long time doesn't necessarily mean the buyer is always happy about it, or satisfied with it. It may only mean that he hasn't gotten around to looking more closely at the competition, or hasn't yet been nudged by his management into doing so.

I've learned that I have to stay alert and attentive to

protect longterm relationships with customers. I have to tell myself that if I don't keep my quality and my service high, the customer may turn to the competition at any moment. I tell myself if I don't keep wooing that customer, no matter how long he's been a customer, I may lose him.

If I'm the seller on the inside of a longterm relationship, I cannot assume the customer is hooked to me and my product forever. But I've made that very mistake, more than once, and regretted it.

By the same token, the seller on the outside of the longterm relationship cannot assume that all is hopeless and that it would be a waste of his time to try to get the business.

The longterm relationship can be cracked and has been, many times. It takes patience and persistence and a kind of piecemeal approach. But it can be done.

But the seller on the outside of the longterm relationship who wants to get his foot, and then his product, in the door had best prepare himself for a long campaign.

I was talking about this at one of our seminars once and made the comment that it can take sales call after sales call for months to drive your wedge into the longterm relationship.

After I said this one of the salesmen attending spoke up: "Five years."

I looked at him. "Do you mean what I think you mean?"

"Yes. I called on a customer regularly for five years before I started to get some of the business that had all been going to another vendor for many years. But once the business started coming, it was well worth the effort."

Too often we sellers look at a prospective customer who's been locked on to another vendor for years and we make one or two calls, then give up. That won't do it. Even if the customer is only moderately satisfied with the product or service he's been buying from the same source for years, it may well be too much trouble to start looking around. That customer has to be wooed.

It's not likely that it will take five years, although even five years of sales calls paid off for that seller at the seminar. It may not take a year, or half a year. But it certainly will take more than a couple of calls to break into that longterm relationship, and probably many more.

Business people are impressed by sales people who really want their business. Going back again and again demonstrates this want. You may go to show the customer samples of your company's product, or service. You may get the customer to visit your plant. You may just stop by and chat about baseball, and the weather, and, by the way, business. But you go back—again and again.

And there's something else: The smartest way to break into that business that's been going to the competitor for so long is to be selfless. Don't go for it all. Go for a small piece of it, to begin with. Even a small piece will give you the opportunity to show the customer what your company, or your product, can do. And it makes life easier for the buyer. He can try you out without taking any big risk.

When we finally changed printers after years we turned to a printing salesman who had been calling on us regularly for months. But, in the beginning, we gave him only an order for a certain size printed envelope—which, incidentally, was all he asked for.

That order enabled him to demonstrate his quality and his service. It wasn't long before he was doing all of our printing.

So don't be a hog. Use a rifle, not a shotgun. Pick out just part of the business you want, and go for that. Pick out that part you can do especially well. If you're a printer and you do high-quality color brochures, go for the brochure order alone. Forget about all the other printing—for the time being. If you finally get the brochure order and you do it better, other business will follow.

Be patient, be persistent, be modest, and you can crack the longterm relationship.

21

Last-Minute Hitches

It happens all the time.

You and the buyer negotiate for days, maybe for weeks. You hammer out each clause of the agreement. You both keep the people in your organizations informed, every step of the way. You finally conclude. You and the buyer feel pretty good about the deal you made.

The agreement is typed up, ready for signatures. It still looks good to the buyer, and to you. At first. Then a period of remorse sets in.

The buyer begins to wonder. Did he pay too much? Should he have held out for better terms? Did he agree too quickly on clause number seven and maybe even clause number eight?

You wonder, too. The deal doesn't look quite as good on paper as it did when you wound up the negotiation. Couldn't you have done a little better?

Real estate brokers will tell you they notice this post-deal remorse, especially on the part of buyers. The principle is simple: Once you have something, it doesn't look quite as good to you.

A husband and wife are delighted when the seller finally agrees to their latest offer for the house. They walk away all smiles. Later, they begin to think. Should they have looked around a little more? Should they have scouted other neighborhoods, other streets?

The important thing is to be prepared for the possibility of last-minute remorse on the buyer's part, and perhaps some on your part, too. Plan for it. Expect it. Don't be surprised by it. Counteract it by reassuring the buyer of the wisdom of the agreement, from his point of view. The remorse will pass.

Be prepared, too, for other last-minute hitches—from the buyer's organization and perhaps from your own. If it's a deal of consequence and the papers go around the circle and up the line in the buyer's organization, critics will come out of the woodwork.

Even though the buyer's people and your people have been kept informed, it will seem as though they didn't really focus on the deal until it was on paper. Then they begin to see possible problems.

Did the buyer think of this or consider that? People in his organization who haven't ventured an opinion or a thought all during the negotiation suddenly pipe up. And maybe some in yours.

There are two things to remember here:

1. Keep your aggravation level down.
2. Keep the deal together.

These last-minute hitches from left field can be very aggravating, can raise your aggravation level suddenly. More aggravation makes you impatient and generally reduces your negotiation skills.

If you fully expect that hitches like this will arise, they will not surprise you if and when they do; they will not raise your aggravation level.

You'll be in a better position to do your job, which is keeping the deal together. You do this with reassurance.

1. Tell the buyer again about your product quality and your service.
2. Tell him about how satisfied other customers are.
3. Tell him how reliable your delivery is, how strong your warranty is, how good the terms are.

Even if you've told him all these things before, and you probably have, tell him again. Go over and over the reasons why his decision was a wise one.

You'll be helping him if you do. You'll be giving him the ammunition he needs to deal with the people of his organization. And you may have to do some reassuring within your own organization as well.

This is a critical period because this is when the people we call the deal killers come out of the ground—and out they come picking.

The buyer's company attorneys start telling him what can go wrong, what legal problems could come up. His procurement review committee tells him he should have done this or insisted upon that, or held out for the other. His quality control people want to know what if the thing falls apart in ten years. His engineers, who may have even checked out the product, ask him what if it doesn't work right. His cost analysts tell him (every time) you can make it for less and still profit.

This is the kind of flak the buyer may be dealing with at the last minute—the kind you have to help him deal with. Again: Expect it, don't be aggravated by it, and you can do a better job of keeping the deal together.

Is there any way to prevent last-minute hitches? A good, strong, detailed contract helps. This brings up the question: Who should write the agreement, or contract?

The answer is *you*. Whenever possible, *you* volunteer to put it all in writing. There are a number of reasons for this.

You take on the job of putting the agreement in writing, and you're relieving the buyer of some work. You're helping him out. Chances are he's overworked, or at least thinks he is, and you're making his life a little easier.

You write the agreement and you can get some other people in your organization involved. This will prevent some static from them later. If they have a hand, they'll help you defend it, rather than pick at it.

You write the agreement and it will reflect your understanding of the deal. No matter how carefully you and the buyer went over the terms and clauses during negotiation, his understanding and your understanding will be just a little different.

Your understanding will prevail if you put the contract together. Your emphasis will prevail. You can stress all the things you're doing for the buyer and his organization; you can emphasize all the positive elements.

You can also make sure the agreement is specific and detailed. And this is important. The more specific the agreement is, the less chance of misunderstanding later.

The more specific it is, the fewer targets for the deal killers to shoot at. It's harder for them to ask what if this and what if that if those what-ifs are all covered in the contract.

And there's something else: If you know ahead of time you'll be writing the agreement, your conversations with the buyer will be clearer. You'll be more specific and you'll elicit more specific responses from him. This will help you write a contract that is specific and detailed.

If it's a prolonged negotiation, which goes through a number of sessions, it's a good idea to take notes along the way. It not only helps later, when you want to put it all into a formal memo or agreement, but helps during the negotiation sessions.

Maybe there are a dozen or more points to negotiate; take them up one at a time or a few at a time. Take notes along the way, on what you and the buyer agree on and on what you don't agree on. Then you can keep his focus on only those things not yet ironed out. That way he doesn't continue to worry about whether or not he wants to make the major decision—to go with your company, your product. You narrow his attention on the delivery or the warranty or the backup service—or whatever seemed to be worrying him the last time you got together.

Keep his attention on the specifics. That way the broad buying decision becomes a foregone conclusion.

Last-minute hitches are facts of life in negotiation. Remember your major weapon in dealing with them—reassuring the buyer he made the right decision. And remember that you have a right to be a broken record. You have a right to tell him again and again things you told him before.

22

Negotiating a Price Increase

We who sell don't like price increases. Nobody can blame us. It's tough negotiating to hold the line on current prices. It's even tougher when management comes along and hikes the prices five or ten percent. We get annoyed, even angry. But we have to deal with the price increase. Our customers get annoyed, some get angry. And we have to deal with them.

Raising prices is never easy. But, done properly, it can be less difficult—much less difficult.

The idea, of course, is to keep your customers. Here are some guidelines to help you do this.

Get all the information you can get. The more you know about the price increase and the reasons for it, the better you will understand it. And the better you will be able to explain it to your customers. If your company holds meetings with sales people to explain the rationale for the price hike, be sure to attend. If you don't understand something, be sure to ask questions. Is the increase related to rising material costs or rising labor costs, or the competition, or the trend of the industry, or the trend of the technology? You should know what factors are relevant to the price increase.

The more you know the better you will be able to plan how you will break the news to your customers, and the better you will be able to deal with their questions.

Give your customers as much advance notice as possible. Buyers must plan. Budgets are drawn up ahead of time. Be sure your customers know about the increase in advance of its effective day, and as much in advance as possible.

One salesman I know makes a practice of passing on rumors of price increases he hears inside his company. "When I hear a rumor that there may be a price increase, I pass that rumor on to my important customers," he told me. "That way, if the rumor is right and an increase is later announced, it's not such a big deal to the buyer. He's been expecting it. He's gotten used to the idea. It makes it easier for me to tell him about it."

Whether you want to pass on such rumors to customers is your business judgment to make. It is important, however, to be sure your customers know well before the effective day so they can plan for it. Inherent here is the concept of acceptance time that we've discussed. The more notice the buyer has that the hike is coming, the more time he has to accept the idea.

Use the power of legitimacy. This way you convey the notion the increase is real, it's official, it's here to stay. Gather every piece of paper you see about the increase: company announcements, press releases, new price lists, memos, letters, whatever. Then when you talk to key customers about the hike, you can show them as well as tell them. This is always more effective.

Present increases to key customers face to face. It's okay to send announcements to smaller customers, perhaps calling them ahead of time to let them know it's coming. But your important customers, you should tell in person, discussing the increase as thoroughly as seems appropriate under the circumstances.

If the customer gets angry, let him. You probably can expect that some customers will get annoyed, upset, even angry. Remember, your price increase is costing the buyer's company money, especially if they're using your product in fixed-price contracts. The buyer has every right to be annoyed.

Co-agonize with the buyer. Don't debate with him. If you do, you give the impression the price increase is open to negotiation. You do not want to give him this impression. You want him to believe the increase is written in concrete, not negotiable. You want him to believe you realize how much it hurts him, and that it hurts you, too. You want him to believe you wish there was something you could do about it, but there just isn't.

Tell the buyer if your management met for months trying to figure out a way to avoid the increase and could not. "There was just no other way," you can say. "We can't keep up the quality of the product or the service without the increase. I hate to be here, and hate to have to tell you this, but there's no choice. We have no choice."

In some circumstances you might say, "We had to raise the price but at least we don't have to drop the line. At least we can still serve you." Raising the possibility that the buyer may not be able to get the product at all may, in some instances, diminish the effect of the increase.

Never tell the buyer the increase isn't that bad. It's always bad for the buyer. Whether it's three percent or 13 percent, it's bad for the buyer. If you tell him it's not that bad, he'll disagree and go on and on about just how bad it is.

Keep higher authority away from your customers. Some companies prepare and send senior sales or management people to help sales persons present and explain price increases to key customers. Unless this is the case, keep higher authority away from your customers. You know your customers, you should be the person who can best handle the announcement and explanation and answer buyer questions. You may well be better at holding the line and not relenting than a senior member of your company would be.

Talk in general terms. Whether you blame the economy or changes in the technology or the competition, talk as generally as possible. Don't be specific. Say, "Our costs are all going up and have been for some time. The company held off the increase as long as it could." If you talk in detailed terms, the customer may suggest how you can economize. If you say heating costs are up, he might suggest you insulate and rescind the increase. If you complain about the rising cost of components, he might suggest that your company look into making the components instead of buying them.

The more generally you talk, the better. And you can exercise your right to be a broken record, repeating the problem of rising costs, shaking your head.

Ask questions. After the customer has gotten over his annoyance or anger and has decided he can't debate your broken record, you can ask questions and make suggestions designed to help him. Can he double or triple his order before the effective date of the increase and save money that way? Can he place larger orders regularly and qualify for a better discount? Can he switch to a cheaper line of the same product? By doing this, you not only show you value the customer's business and want to keep it. You also show that you want to help him get a better deal, that you're willing to negotiate everything but the price increase. And you may end up with more business than you had before the increase.

Delay the price increase only as a last resort. And do it carefully. You can probably put off the effective date of the increase 30 or 60 days if you decide it's entirely necessary to keep a good customer. When you do, however, get a letter from the buyer or some written acknowledgment of the new price and its effective date. The point is, get the new price on the record or the customer may want the old price again next time he orders.

Another way to do this is to say, "Okay, you want 400 units. I'll give you 390 at the old price if you'll take the other ten at the new price." That way the new price is in the books.

If you manage sales people, prepare them. If you're an executive or manager of sales representatives, arm them thoroughly to present the increase to their customers. Explain every aspect of the increase, every factor involved in the decision to raise the price.

Once at a seminar we had sales people from three divisions of an electronic parts company, divisions that sold different product lines. The company had recently announced an across-the-board price increase.

The sales people of two of the three divisions, those headquartered in Boston and Chicago, were very well informed about the increase, accepted it, defended it. Those from the other division, headquartered in Phoenix, complained about it, resented it, resisted it, fought it.

I learned in conversation after the seminar that the Boston and Chicago divisions had sent a top executive to meet with sales people and in each case he spent an entire morning with them. He explained the increase thoroughly; he answered their questions. The Phoenix division had sent a lower level employee with a box containing the new price lists. He passed out the lists to the sales people and in ten minutes was gone.

The difference is obvious: the first two divisions used the power of commitment. They took the time and trouble to explain the increase to their people; in effect, to sell it to them. The other division dropped it and ran. And it would be months before the sales reps of that other division learned to live with the price hike.

23

Tactics to Watch Out For

Some buyer tactics demand special alertness on the part of the seller. You have to watch out for them, be ready to confront them when they crop up. They are ethical. But some can also be unethical, or somewhere in between—depending on how they are used. Where they fall on the moral scale is not important, however. The important thing is that we have to deal with them. Here they are:

GOOD-GUY-BAD-GUY

Hollywood likes this one, and you've seen it a hundred times in crime movies. Police track down a suspect and arrest him. One very tough detective hauls him into an interrogation room and hammers questions at him, over and over. The tough cop acts like he's convinced the sus-

189

pect is guilty, convinced he only has to wear him down. He shouts at him, threatens him, maybe even shoves him around or starts to beat him up.

Then enters the other detective—the nice guy. He ushers the bad detective out of the room, maybe pushes him out angrily. Then he sits down quietly, smiles, and offers the suspect a cup of coffee or a cigarette. He talks softly to the suspect, tells him he wants to help him, wants to make it easy for him. Before long the suspect is telling all he knows.

In negotiation, the good-guy-bad-guy routine takes a generally similar shape. The bad guy may be another buyer, the buyer's boss, an attorney, a cost analyst, an accountant, almost anyone from the buyer's organization.

At first, the bad guy does all the talking. The other person usually sits there quietly, smiling. The bad guy goes on and on—making demands, unreasonable demands, perhaps outrageous demands. Still, the good guy just sits.

After some time the bad guy finally stops talking. Maybe he gets up and leaves the room. Then the good guy starts. He's polite, he's friendly. After listening to the other loudmouth he seems like a swell guy. After listening to the bad guy's unreasonable demands, his demands seem perfectly reasonable. He's such a pleasure to deal with that you give in—unless you recognize the tactic at the outset.

The earlier you do spot the good-guy-bad-guy tactic the more you neutralize the bad guy's mouthings. Don't get aggravated, don't argue, don't debate, just sit and listen. Let him talk himself tired. Then, when the time comes, deal with the good guy. But—consider the good guy's demands without comparing them to the bad guy's demands. If you don't, tough demands made softly by the good guy may seem easy in relation to the other guy's.

Ann Douglas studied labor relations for some years and wrote about what she called "oratorial fireworks," using the example of a negotiator playing bad guy.

Union negotiators would sit down with management negotiators and almost immediately one of the union representatives would begin a tirade. He would rant and rave—going back to the 1920s and 1930s—about how management treated labor badly. He would go on and on, gradually working up to the 1950s and 1960s, and current times.

Then the demands would come—every demand in the book.

Why did he go through all this? As he explained it, he was not really talking to the management negotiator across the table. He was talking to that negotiator's people, and to his own people.

"The tougher I am, the tougher negotiation his people will expect, and the easier it will be for him to say yes as we get down to real negotiating. I'm making it easier for him to say yes to me. As for my own people, they'll never forgive me if I don't make every demand. They'll forgive me if I don't get them, but they won't forgive me if I don't make them."

In sales negotiation the good-guy-bad-guy tactic works because the bad guy's routine reduces your aspiration level and makes the good guy's position look inviting. First thing you know you're agreeing to terms that are tough but don't appear to be so.

After you identify the tactic and decide to let the bad guy go on and on until he finally runs out of breath, you can deal with the good guy on a rational level.

If the situation gets so out of hand it is impossible for you to deal with it, you have the right to protest to higher authority. Upper management doesn't like its people to be bad guys, or at least doesn't like to hear about it. Going up the line may mean a change of negotiators on the other side, a change that is to your benefit.

WHAT-IF

This tactic can drive a sales person crazy. But it won't if the sales person remembers the importance of time, and of taking time before responding. And sometimes the sales person can turn the tactic to his advantage—getting a larger order than either he or the buyer figured on.

Buyers use this tactic to get more information about the selling organization: its costs, its pricing, its profits. Sellers must be cautious or they will find themselves doling out far more information than they should.

The tactic goes this way:

A buyer needs 1000 components. But he doesn't ask for a bid on 1000 components. He asks for bids on 100, 1000, 10,000, and maybe more. Or he may initially ask for the bid on 1000 units. Then, after getting it, he may ask: What if we buy 5000? . . . what if we buy 10,000?

Armed with bids for a range of quantities, a buyer and a competent cost analyst can learn many things. They can estimate production costs, production capacity, pricing policies, and even margins of profit. This information, of course, strengthens the buyer's position in negotiation.

We have a friend with a tailoring business who buys a good deal of material. He always pays by cash or check, never asks for credit, and this is his what-if routine.

He needs 1000 yards of a certain material. He goes to

the material house, and the dialogue goes something like
this:

"How much is it if I buy 1000 yards?"

"Twelve dollars a yard."

"What if I take 5000 yards?"

"Eleven dollars a yard."

"How much of this material do you have on hand?"

"About 25,000 yards."

"Suppose I take all of it—paying cash—what is the
price?"

"Eight dollars a yard, if you take all."

Our tailor friend now knows that the material man can
sell that material at $8 a yard and still make a profit. Once
he has gotten that number, the $8, into the negotiation,
the original $12 and later $11 never come up again. He
begins negotiating from the $8.

And usually he ends up getting his original 1000 yards
at a price much closer to the $8 than to the $12.

There are other what-if questions that buyers use. For
example:

- What if we place the order when your factory is
  slow?
- What if we agree to a one-year contract?
- What if we take your total production?
- What if we supply the material?
- What if we forget about the warranty?
- What if we buy nuts and bolts instead of just nuts?
- What if we pay part in advance, and progress pay-
  ments?
- What if we give you technical help?
- What if we simplify the specifications by doing
  this?

The answers to all such what-ifs as these give the buyer more information about your business, more insight into how your organization does business.

When dealing with what-ifs, don't answer quickly, and answer carefully. Take time, tell him you'll have to get back to him, consult with others in your organization if necessary.

Probe to find out what the buyer really needs, what he really intends to order. Again, this takes time, and patience. And it's information you may have to get not from the buyer but from someone in his engineering production department.

The what-if *can* work in your favor. Even though a buyer may set out wanting 1000 units, or just a one-year contract, your answer to his what-if may turn the order into 3000 units, or a three-year contract—with terms that make it a better deal for both of you.

LOST MEMOS, EXPOSED NOTES, FORGOTTEN BRIEFCASES

This is a tricky one, and you never can be sure about it. But you should always be wary of it. It's used not only in business but in diplomatic circles and in politics.

I have a friend who was a newspaperman for many years and he once told me how politicians or politicians' aides used this tactic to "leak" stories to the press.

"It's something I ran into a number of times over the years—in the offices of politicians on the state level and in Washington," he said.

"Let's say you're interviewing the person, or maybe just talking, just making conversation.

"At a certain point he makes an excuse and says he has to leave for a few minutes and you're alone in his office, sitting on the other side of his desk.

"You're a reporter. Naturally, you're nosey. You're always on the lookout for a story, or a lead. Your eyes wander across his desk. Suddenly you see a letter, or a report, or a memo. You begin to read and you know right away that it's something the guy—supposedly—would not want you to see. But it is, at the same time, information that sounds like a good story or a lead for a good story.

"The journeyman reporter learns to be very wary in this situation, because it's a favorite way for politicians to leak stories that they don't want to be linked to, but that will have some political advantage for them if they appear.

"It may be the guy just plain forgot what was on his desk. But it may be he intended for you to read the thing and rush back to your desk and write the story—attributing 'confidential sources' or something like that.

"I didn't ignore the situation. But I was very careful. If it was information that led to a story I checked things very carefully. I didn't want to miss a good story. But I didn't want to be used by some guy to serve his selfish purpose."

Dr. Karrass in his Effective Negotiating® seminar tells about a man he knew who got machine shop work from a large aerospace corporation and subcontracted the jobs to smaller outfits at lower prices.

Whenever a prospective bidder came to this man's office, the bidder would accidentally find a handwritten list of presumably competitive bids.

"All the prospective bidder had to do was bid lower than the lowest bid on the list to get the job," Dr. Karrass says. "The truth was that the list was a false plant meant to be read while the buyer momentarily left the room on some false pretense. This man found that bidders invariably bid lower than the make-believe low bid on the list."

Beware of buyers who leave the room, leaving behind exposed information they presumably wouldn't want you to have. While you're straining to read upside down, you may be falling into a trap. If you're negotiating somewhere on neutral ground, beware of buyers who leave open briefcases on the table when they leave the room for awhile. Their contents may have been designed especially for your prying eyes.

Good information is rarely that easy to get.

LOWBALLING

Lowballing is a questionable tactic we usually associate with shady sales people. They go into a deal with a very low price, the buyer agrees, then come add-ons, extras, changes that hike up the final price.

But some buyers also use the lowballing tactic.

They lowball with promises of big future orders to come, big orders that never materialize.

They lowball with easy specifications that are later changed and made more complicated, more costly to produce.

They lowball by promising to pay in ten days or 30 days—then paying in 60 or 90 days.

They lowball by giving the seller all the time in the world for delivery—then demanding the product the next week.

They get you locked up—signed on the dotted line—then make more and more demands.

How do you protect yourself against this tactic? Most important is to try to determine before concluding the negotiation precisely what the buyer's real needs and wants are and what changes might come up later, and to provide for possible changes in your terms.

Pay little or no attention to promises of huge orders somewhere out there in the future. This kind of talk is especially cheap and, as the ancient Chinese said, "Talk doesn't cook rice."

Try to determine before the negotiation how faithfully the buyer's organization lives up to its commitment to pay bills in a certain time, and lives up to other terms.

Make the contract or agreement as detailed as possible, to cover demand or request situations that may possibly arise in the future. As we noted earlier, the more detailed the agreement, the less chance of misunderstanding—and the more protected you are against this kind of lowballing.

Be prepared to walk away from the deal, if you have an out. Nobody wants to pass up or lose business. But there is business that is not worth the trouble it becomes, quite literally.

FAIT ACCOMPLI

Something done is usually difficult to undo. That's the power of fait accompli—accomplished fact. And some buyers will use it to their advantage.

What we sales people have to remember is that a check

is very hard to return, and a signed contract is difficult to return. That works against us.

Let's say you sell a machine for $900. Then, after you bill the customer for $900 he sends you a paid-in-full check for $860. Are you going to send the check back? Probably not. Chances are you'll deposit the check and forget about it, or you'll call the customer and try to negotiate the other $40, and perhaps end up with something between $860 and $900.

Suppose you and the buyer agree on price and terms and delivery. You agree that the price will be $1 a pound, the terms will be 30 days, delivery will be four weeks. Then the buyer sends you a purchase order. It says $1 a pound, but it lists 60 days for payment and two weeks for delivery. Will you return the signed purchase order? Not likely. You'll contact the buyer and try to negotiate the terms and delivery or you'll just accept them as stipulated in the order.

Here's another one. Your invoice says the customer may deduct two percent if the bill is paid in ten days. The customer takes 30 days to pay the bill, but deducts the two percent anyway. Is that check difficult to return? Certainly.

REVERSE AUCTION

This tactic is a kind of trap, one to beware. It goes this way:

A man decides he wants to build a swimming pool. He decides he wants one 15 by 30 feet, going to a depth of 9 feet, and he wants it by a certain date. His specifications seem simple enough to him. He asks three pool companies for bids.

He gets his bids, he looks them over, and he discovers there are substantial differences. One salesman has proposed a certain kind of filter system, different from the others. The second bidder has a different coping and deck.

The buyer calls all three bidders. He asks one to come to his house at nine the next morning, the other to come at nine-fifteen, and the other at nine-thirty. They arrive one by one and he shows them into his living room and lets them sit around together for awhile.

At ten o'clock the buyer asks the first sales person to come into his den office. They go over that sales person's bid. In the course of the conversation, the bidder mentions his competitors in the other room.

"I see you're getting bids from others, including Joe out there. His pools are okay, but I hear lately they've been having a lot of trouble with their filter systems. Just thought you'd want to know that." In the course of the talk over his proposal, the first bidder also decides he can lower his price, shave it by ten percent, and he tells the buyer that.

The buyer thanks the first vendor and asks the second one to come into his office. They go over that proposal in detail. Then the second sales person comments, "Sam, who was just in here, is an old friend of mine. I'm sorry his company is having so much financial trouble. I understand they've got a lot of empty holes around the city—jobs they haven't finished." The second seller doesn't lower his price. But he does the same thing. He voluntarily throws in a jacuzzi at the end of the pool, without charge.

And so it goes with the third sales person. He knocks his price down and badmouths both the other sellers.

Now, what has the buyer done with this reverse-auction tactic? He's done several things.

He's thrown the sellers together. This puts them under strong competitive pressure. Being aware of the competition is one thing. Sitting in the same room with a couple of competitors, waiting to go over your proposal for the same job, increases the competitive pressure enormously. Sellers who usually resist lowering prices may do so under such circumstances as these. Sellers who usually avoid bad-mouthing the competition may do so under these circumstances.

The buyer has learned things. After going over the vendors' proposals with them, one by one, he knows more about what he's buying—the filter system, the heating systems, tile and coping, and so on. He's also heard some words of warning from the sellers about the others.

After the reverse auction, the buyer knows more about pool specifications, and can write his again more specifically if he so desires. The buyer also has new prices from the vendors that are lower than those originally submitted. He has a better fix on how far he can push them, how low they can go and still make a profit.

This tactic is used in large-scale negotiations, too.

In one case, a government agency asked several aerospace companies to submit bids by a certain date on a multimillion-dollar project. The companies assigned teams of negotiators, met with the government representatives, and submitted their proposals.

The team of buyers gathered the bids, studied them, and—armed with their enhanced knowledge—rewrote their specifications. They then gave their new, tighter, smarter specifications to the aerospace representatives and asked for new proposals to be submitted at a new date.

The government buyers had used the first set of bids to learn more about what they were buying, heightened the feeling of competitive pressure on the part of the vendors, and ended up with lower prices.

How do you, the seller, protect yourself against this tactic?

1. *You can refuse to take part.* It's a tough situation for the sales person to be in; the temptation to lower prices and lower prices again is very strong. The business may not be worth it.
2. *You can take part, but arrange to be the last seller seen by the buyer.* This has several advantages. One is that, if you're last, you probably will learn something about what went on between the buyer and the sellers who preceded you. This enhances your power of knowledge—always an edge in negotiation. Another advantage in being last is that, by the time he sees you, the buyer is tired of the whole thing, anxious to wind up the deal and go on to something else. And still another advantage is that the buyer tends to remember best what went on in his meeting with the last bidder.
3. *You can arrange to bring with you the most capable and articulate technical support person available in your organization.* This gives you added strength, and added credibility.
4. *You can have a bottom line.* Decide before you take part just how much you'll go down in your price, and don't swerve from that decision. Experience shows that we sales people, when we find ourselves in the reverse-auction kind of situation, tend to give away much too much.

When you realize that a buyer is using this tactic and you decide to go for the business anyway, be sure to prepare. Buy as much time as you can to plan your counter-measures. If the buyer asks you to come by at nine a.m. Monday, try saying, "I can't make that, but how about nine a.m. Wednesday or Thursday?" He may say fine, pick your day. He may mention other useful information regarding other appointments with other vendors.

As we all know, the later in the day the better to see a buyer, and the later in the week the better to see a buyer. Ten o'clock Monday morning, when the buyer is off and running with the new week is not nearly as good as four o'clock Friday afternoon, when the buyer is tired and daydreaming about the upcoming weekend.

ESCALATING AUTHORITY

Car dealers are famous for this one. You negotiate with a car salesman and make a deal. Then he says, "Oh, by the way, the manager has to approve it." And he disappears.

A few minutes later he returns with the sad news. The manager says he has to get $500 more for the car. So you're back negotiating again and you end up paying, if not $500 more, something more.

The salesman has dealt with you as if he had the authority to make the deal. Then, after making it, he tells you, in effect, he didn't have the authority and has to go up the line. It's a tactic, an old one. And one that some buyers use, too.

One case I know involves the president and vice president of a small company.

The vice president, a tough guy, is first to negotiate

with sales people. He hammers at them, he makes very tough demands, he treats them rudely.

After awhile the president comes into the picture. He gives the vice president a tongue-lashing for his ill behavior, sends him out of the room, then sits down with the sales person.

"That guy is a lot of trouble. I probably ought to get rid of him," the president tells the sales person. "I apologize for his behavior. But you know . . . about these terms, he does have a point." And he goes on to negotiate.

This is an example of escalating authority, seasoned with the good-guy-bad-guy routine.

The most flagrant authority example I know involves four brothers who are in the movie business. They negotiate with stars or, more accurately, stars' agents. And big stars mean big money.

The youngest brother usually starts the negotiation with the agent. Then, after awhile, the second youngest brother takes over. He really should have been doing it from the start, he explains to the agent.

First thing the agent knows, the second brother is gone from the scene and the next older brother is dealing with him—starting from scratch. By this time the agent is getting worn down, weary, and his aspiration level has dropped substantially.

Next time the agent appears for the continuance of the negotiation, the fourth, the oldest brother, is there, all apologies for not having dealt with the agent from the start. Then the oldest brother goes back to the beginning, starts negotiating from point one.

I don't have to tell you how the agent feels by this time. His aspiration level is somewhere around his shoes, he's tired of the whole thing, he just wants to make the deal and get out.

How do you protect yourself against this tactic?

Most important, of course, is to try to find out as early as possible if the buyer you're dealing with actually has the authority to make the deal.

Here's one way:

The buyer makes several demands. You respond by saying, "If we meet those demands, can we close the deal today—right now?"

If he starts hemming and hawing, making excuses, then chances are he doesn't have the authority. And you know you're going to end up dealing with someone else, someone who does have the authority.

And what does this also mean? It means you should avoid playing all your cards at one time. Save some for the next person you'll be confronting.

As a matter of fact, this is a good general rule in negotiation. Try to get the other party to make his demands first—all of them. But play your cards slowly. If you have seven points that make up your position, use one or two, then wait. When necessary, use another one or two. Then, the balance, as necessary. If you do this, and you do get escalated up the line, from one buyer to another, or to his manager, you have ammunition in store.

24

The Sales Person's Bill of Rights

Have you ever punished yourself later because you didn't have the answer on the tip of your tongue when the buyer asked the question? Or because at another point you hesitated, didn't know what to say, and ended up saying nothing? Or because you answered a question and it turned out later you were wrong?

Well, stop berating yourself. It doesn't do any good, it crimps your negotiating skills. And besides, you have the right to do all of those things.

There is what we call the sales person's bill of rights. They are things it's okay to do in negotiation, sometimes smart to do. Here they are:

You have the right to be wrong.

Nobody's infallible, nobody's right all the time. You make a mistake, you give a wrong answer, don't punish yourself. We all do it. Just fix it. Call the guy and say, "Joe,

I'm sorry. I gave you some bum information. The machine doesn't do 1300 lines a minute. It's closer to 1200, actually about 1190. I don't know where I got the 1300 but it's wrong. Sorry."

Joe will appreciate your honesty in admitting the mistake, respect you for correcting it, and think all the more of you because of it. There's no reason to stew about it. You fix it, forget it, and go on to more productive things.

You have the right to be indecisive.

You've heard that the sharp businessperson makes decisions in split seconds, that it's the mark of the person headed for the top? Forget it. In negotiation, you have every right to put off a decision, to hem and haw, shuffle your feet, and say, "I don't know. I'll have to think about it. I don't know."

The fact is, being indecisive may be the smartest move to make under certain circumstances. Have you ever negotiated with someone who kept saying, "I don't know. I don't know. I don't know." It wears you down, tries your patience, and the first thing you know you're giving in, just so you don't have to listen to the guy say, "I don't know" any more.

You have the right to ask questions the buyer has no right to answer.

Go ahead and ask them. Maybe he shouldn't answer them. But maybe he will. It couldn't hurt to ask. How do the other bids look? He shouldn't tell you about other bids, but he might. He might even show them to you. It's happened, many times.

Does he have a lot of pressure from his boss to get this

deal settled so he can move on to other buys? He may say he sure does. How do his engineers rate your product in comparison to the competition? He probably shouldn't tell you, but he may very well tell you they love your product.

When we're asked a direct question, it's difficult not to answer, even if we shouldn't. Buyers frequently answer questions they have no right to answer. So ask.

You have the right to be a pest, to be annoyingly persistent.

If you have a good product and you're convinced you can serve the buyer well, better than he's being served, call on him repeatedly. Don't say to yourself, "Well, I saw him twice and he's just not interested," and forget about him. Call again and again. He will get the impression you really want his business, and he will get the impression you're committed to the quality of your product or service and the reliability of your organization.

You have the right to be silent, not to answer a question, not to talk.

Often, if you don't respond to the buyer's comment or question, he will after a moment fill the silence. He probably will repeat what he said, with further elaboration, with more information. And, because of your silence, you learn more and more, which is to your advantage in the negotiation. Also, remaining silent for awhile gives you more time to think, more time to decide on your next move. And time, as we've said repeatedly, is money in negotiation.

You have the right to be a broken record.

Sometimes you don't know what to say but feel you have to say something. Say what you said before. Say the same things again and again. You may be repeating yourself because you don't know what else to say. But the buyer may become increasingly impressed because of your repetition. He may become increasingly impressed with your conviction.

You have the right to test a deadline, and the right to negotiate to extend it.

Some deadlines are real. Others aren't. You have the right to probe, to determine if the deadline is, indeed, a real one. And you have the right to determine if the deadline can be extended.

You've had buyers tell you they needed your lowest price by Friday—and two weeks later you and the buyer were still negotiating. Obviously, the deadline wasn't real. Or, if real, he was able to stretch it. If you think you need more time to respond to the buyer's query, ask for more time. If he says he needs your proposal by January 3, you have the right to say, "I'd really like to have a little more time, to do it properly. Would it be okay if I had it on January 6?" He may say no, the deadline is firm. But he may say sure, take a few more days. It can do no harm to ask and it can help.

You have the right to be dumb.

You try to do it in an intelligent way, of course, but you have the right to be ignorant, not to know. The less information the buyer has, the better it is for you in the negotiation. If he asks you to break out the cost of the materials in your product, you have the right to say, "Gee, I ought to know those figures, but I just don't. They change all the time and I don't take time to keep up with them as well as I should."

All these things that you can do or not do, say or not say, are your rights as a sales person. Some are also, as you see, useful seller tactics and countermeasures to buyer tactics in negotiation.

When the occasion calls for it, exercise your rights.

25

Summing Up

This is, as you see, the closing chapter. It's the end of the book. But it's the beginning for you—as someone now armed with the strategies, tactics, techniques, and skills of effective negotiation.

This is a summing-up chapter. Quickly and succinctly, we're going to step through the major points of the book. These are the things you should remember if you want to put the contents of this book to work for you, in all areas of your life. They'll be a way to keep this book working for you in the months and years to come.

Here they are—the guidelines for effective negotiation.

Aim Higher   Always aim higher in negotiation, and you'll come out better. Experience and research have proved this over and over, time and time again. Remember, your job works against you here. You hear your prices are too high, your competition too good, your product not good enough. Turn a deaf ear to these comments. Keep reminding yourself they're just tactics, ways to get your price down. Aim higher; you can always come down if you must.

Remember Your Power   Power is what you think it is. It's in the mind. Go over all the possible powers you might have going for you before any negotiation. Don't think about the limitations on your power. Think about the limitations on the buyer's power—his pressures, his problems. Remember the Paradox of Power that's been demonstrated so many times. One person with real power doesn't realize it and goes into the negotiation timid and intimidated. Another person with little or no real power goes in demonstrating strength and vigor. The second one does better. Why? Because power is in the mind.

Use Wooing   Remember your power of wooing, no matter how good business is. The more business you want, the more you will get. Woo the customer, impress him with how much you want the business. That's *want*, not need. Never need the business but always want it. Remember, too, that work can be part of the power of wooing. Do your homework, show the customer you made extra efforts to get his business.

Take Risks   Being willing to take risks is a power for you in negotiation. How much you can risk is a business judgment. Remember, there are a great many risks buyers won't take. And the larger the buyer's organization, the more risks he won't take. Be willing to gamble for a better deal.

Use Legitimacy   The printed price list, the printed discount sheet, the published credit policy, the standard form, the regular procedure—all these can work for you. If your published policy states you cannot give more than 30 days credit, the buyer will accept it quicker than he will accept your word for it. And you're not his adversary. Your printed credit policy sheet is his adversary. It's in print, so it must be true. Legitimacy is a strong source of power for you.

Use Your Competition   Instead of fretting over your competition, concentrate on all the possible limitations on the customer's ability to use your competition. Maybe the customer had a bad experience with that competition. Maybe the competitor can't deliver on time, or can't give the needed credit, or has a bad reputation, or doesn't service his product, or, for that matter, can't even provide the product. Dwell on all the possible problems your buyer may have with your competitors.

Be Committed and Use Customer Commitment   The more you're committed to the worth of your product, the reliability of your service, the good reputation of your company, the more powerful you are. Be committed, too, to your own goals and targets. Use commitment from persons in the buying organization. Once someone in the customer organization has expressed his commitment to your product or your company he won't go back on his own word. He'll back you up.

Use Knowledge   The more you know about your company, your product, and your industry, the better off you

are in negotiation. The more you know about the customer
and his organization, the stronger you are. The more you
know about your competition, the better for you. Knowing how to listen, how to lead the other person on—to talk
and to tell—is important. The other side of this is control-
ling knowledge about your organization that flows to the
buying organization. The less the buyer knows about your
company's internal workings, the better.

Take Time Time is money. The more time you take in
negotiation, the more money you come out with. There's
no hurry. Take time to discover your powers. Take time
to discover the buyer's real wants and needs. Take time to
consider the other person's tactics, and how to counteract
them. Remember the slogan: *Befriend Time.*

Know When to Shut Up Do you want the customer to
know you have an oversized inventory? Of course not.
But we've all made dumb remarks. Being careful to avoid
dumb remarks is an important rule. Tell others in your
organization to shut up. The other side of this one: listening for dumb remarks on the part of the other person. He
may tell you he's desperate for your product. He may tell
you your product is the best by far. He may even tell you
how other vendors bid.

Beware of Garbage and the Garbage Truck If you're constantly looking and listening for disparaging remarks about
your company and your product, you'll find them. If you're
looking for compliments about your competition you'll
find them. It's the buyer's job to help you find them. You
see what you look for, you hear what you listen for. Keep

your senses tuned to the positive. Don't look for the garbage. Remember, there's always a truck going to the garbage dump—if you want to get on it. Keep the positive ideas and information about your company and product in your head. Turn a deaf ear to the rest.

Spot Tactics As Tactics   When the buyer says that's all the money she has in the budget, or tells you to take or leave her offer, or says something like "you gotta do better than that," identify her move as a tactic and deal with it as a tactic. Don't get angry, don't get upset, don't get discouraged; simply make your move to counteract her tactic, to get her thinking closer to your thinking, her offer closer to your price.

Don't Forget: Forever Can Be for Now   When the other person in the negotiation says, "Ten dollars a unit is as high as I can go, that's the limit, that's my last and final offer," he may well mean it, at the moment. It is true in his mind forever, but forever-for-now. Negotiation is in constant motion and things are constantly changing. Ten minutes later in the same negotiation he may say $11 a unit is his last and final offer and in his mind that figure is true forever, but forever-for-now. Always say no once more before saying yes.

Anything the Result of Negotiation Can Be Renegotiated
If you're told the figure in the budget is written in concrete, it might be. But it might not be. It was the result of an internal negotiation, and anything the result of negotiation can be renegotiated. And there are things other

than price to be negotiated which can be to your advantage: the payment terms, the specifications, the packaging, the service, the training.

Remember the Satisfiers   The buyer talks about price, price, price, but he has many other wants and needs. And the more of these other wants and needs you satisfy, the higher the price he will pay. He wants to avoid risk and worry about products and service; he wants to be considered fair, nice, competent, with good taste; he wants to look good in his own organization; he wants to add to his knowledge; he wants to get the purchase over with and move on to the next one. The more time you spend on these wants and the less time you spend on price, the more he will pay.

Concede to Get Most Satisfaction   It's not *how much* you concede but *how* you concede that counts. The buyer who has to work a little for a small discount goes away from the negotiation feeling better than the one who got a big discount with a word. Concede slowly, a little at a time, in small and, when possible, diminishing increments. Don't be the first to concede on major issues. Beware of conceding too much as the deadline nears. Always try to get something in return when you concede. Try to get the most buyer satisfaction for each concession.

Leave the Customer Feeling He Got a Bargain   You don't achieve this with price only. If he paid less than the going price or less than the printed price, he will, of course, get the bargain feeling. He will also get the bargain feeling if he thinks he got the last one, or got one that someone else wanted, or got one that has very high performance and a very good service record. He will get the feeling of the bargain if the product brings him compliments on his judgment or taste.

Negotiate Funny Money Carefully   If you're conceding in terms of free service or free delivery or free manuals or deferred payment or longer credit or free advertising, you're negotiating funny money. And you have to watch it. Translate it into real value—dollars whenever possible— to get the most customer satisfaction for the concession. Two free service calls? Send the customer a service bill for what you would normally cost and mark it "paid" or "complimentary," or something. Then he'll know the real value. If you're dealing in a unit cost, that can even be funny money. Don't think about the penny a pound, think about the total that penny represents for the total order. You'll negotiate better.

Strive for the Better Deal for Both Parties   You want to leave the negotiation feeling good, feeling you got a good deal. You also want the other person to leave the negotiation feeling good, feeling he got a good deal. Every negotiation affects every other negotiation. If he feels good when you close, he will want to do business with you again. Look upon negotiation as farming a relationship, not hunting. Always asking for something in return helps make it a better deal for both parties. Concede the five percent on the price if he'll pick up the merchandise. Agree to the longer pay period if he'll increase the volume of the order. He gets his discount, you get something in

return. It helps build the both-win kind of negotiation—
the quality negotiation.

Don't Ignore the Longterm Relationship   Whether you're
on the inside or the outside, you shouldn't neglect the
longterm relationship. The customer you've had for years
deserves more attention, not less. The customer who has
been buying from your competitor for years may be perfectly happy. She may also be very unhappy, but just hasn't
gotten around to doing anything about it. Persistence
pays off when trying to break into the competitor's longterm relationship. Selflessness pays off. Go for a part of
the competitor's business with the longterm customer,
start off by going after just a piece of the action. It may
lead to all of it.

Watch Out for Last-Minute Problems   The agreement has
been reached, it's being typed, it's all set to go, and some
deal killer comes out of left field. The buyer's legal guy
or his cost analyst or his superior starts nit-picking, finding fault, Monday morning quarterbacking. Expect the
last-minute hitch, prepare for it, and it's less likely to try
your patience and raise your aggravation level. Constantly
reassure the buyer of the wisdom of his decision, tell him
again how good your company and product and service
are. Help him deal with his deal killer to keep the deal together.

Write the Contract   Whenever possible, volunteer to
write the agreement or contract. You'll be relieving the
buyer of some work and there are other advantages. It
will represent your understanding of the deal. It will em-

phasize those things *you* want to emphasize. Make it as specific as possible, down to the smallest detail. The more specific it is, the less chance for misunderstanding later.

Negotiate the Price Increase with Care　Get all the information you can from your company about why the price is being hiked. Tell the customer in person, if possible, or by phone. Give the customer as much advance notice as possible. Give him or her the reasons, in general terms, and be prepared to answer questions. Present it as an accomplished fact, not open to negotiation. You don't like it any more than the buyer does. Co-agonize with the customer. Ask questions: Can he increase his order and get a quantity discount, for example?

Beware of Certain Tactics　If the buyer only needs 100 units and wants to know what they would cost if he bought 1000 or 10,000, watch out. He may try to get the 100 for the unit price of the large order. If he tries to get your price down by promising huge additional orders sometime off in the future, ignore the promises. If the customer tries to play you against your competitors, don't fall for it. He may well be doing the same thing to them. If buyers pull a good-guy-bad-guy routine on you, be careful. The bad guy will make the good guy seem easier to deal with than he really is.

Remember Your Rights　You have the right to be wrong, as long as you correct your mistake. You have the right to hem and haw, drag your feet, take time to think. You have the right to get persistent, the right to be a broken record, the right to test a deadline and negotiate to extend it, and the right to play dumb when you want to. Know these rights and you won't be pushed into a closing that's not good for you and not good for the other party, either. The last thing to remember before you go into a negotiation: your Bill of Rights.

ABOUT THE AUTHOR

GARY KARRASS is a recognized national authority on negotiation and, especially, negotiation from the sales side.

For the past ten years he has been Chief Executive of the Los Angeles–based Karrass Seminars Inc. and Karrass International, and he is Vice President of the Center for Effective Negotiating.

Mr. Karrass is the originator and designer of the widely praised and most successful Effective *Sales* Negotiating® seminar, now titled Negotiate to Close. He formulated this program in response to numerous requests from company presidents, sales management people, and sales people who expressed their need for a seminar that dealt with negotiation strictly from the sales point of view.

Over the course of the past decade, Mr. Karrass has conducted his Effective *Sales* Negotiating seminar and general Effective Negotiating seminar for company presidents, executives, managers, and sales, purchasing, and technical people of more than 170 of the Fortune 500 leading industrial organizations in the United States, as well as for scores of smaller business organizations and other groups.

During his years of conducting negotiation seminars, Mr. Karrass has also delivered numerous speeches on the subject before business and professional groups. He has earned a reputation as an extremely informative, inspiring—and entertaining—public speaker, and has been presented with a number of awards for his speaking appearances.